Options Trading

2 Books in 1: Discover How to Make Money from Home. Learn Fundamental and Technical Analysis to Become a Successful Trader.

Andrew Bennett

TABLE OF CONTENTS

PART 1

Options Trading

The Ultimate Guide to Make Money Online Investing in Stock Market. Discover the Benefits of Technical Analysis, Financial Leverage and Risk Management to Generate Passive Income

Andrew Bennett

Introduction

Stock options and futures are the frequently discussed investment products that people are accustomed to reading about on the market news. In the morning, several professional buyers and traders wake up and look at stock futures to get a feel when the market begins compared to the end of the previous day. In order to see whether profits can be gained by hedging their bets during the trading day, some can look at the price of oil contracts or other commodities.

You might presume that these futures contracts or options markets are another advanced financial tool developed for their disingenuous intentions by Wall Street gurus, but if you did, you would be wrong. In reality, contracts for options and futures did not exist at all on Wall Street. These devices date back hundreds of years to their origins-well before they formally started selling in 1973.

The advent of Futures for Commodity

A futures contract requires the investor to acquire or exchange a given amount of a product at a specified price within a specified time period. Energy, grain, natural gas, wheat, copper, potash, and several other highly traded properties are commodities. These products are extensively used by a large spectrum of market players, starting from Wall Street investors to cultivators who want their agricultural products to generate stable money.

The development of the first completely functioning commodity exchange in the late seventeenth century is attributed to the Japanese. The samurai were paid in rice, not money, for their contributions during this time span. Naturally, they decided to regulate the rice markets, where the rice exchange and trading took place. The samurai had the option to generate a profit on a more stable basis by setting up a regulated market in which sellers and buyers could 'barter' for rice. The samurai began the "Dojima Rice Trade" in 1697, working with other rice brokers. That scheme was quite dissimilar to the Kansai Derivative Trade, the new Japanese agricultural trade.

This book, besides delving into the functions of the Options market, shall touch upon important information with regard to options trading. However, the most important and interesting feature of this book is that, as you read through, it will discuss and describe in detail various trading strategies that will help you to extend your earning potential through the employment of anxiety-free smart options trading techniques.

CHAPTER 1: History of Options Trading

Modern option contracts are generally related to equities. What is a stock option, then, and where did it come from? Simply put, over a defined time frame, a stock option contract grants the holder the right to buy or sell a defined number of shares for a pre-determined price.

In comparison to other traditional types, like buying shares, many people think of trading of options as a relatively new form of investment. As we know, modern options contracts were only really instituted when the Chicago Board of Options Exchange (CBOE) was established, but it is believed that the fundamental concept of options deals was built in Ancient Greece: maybe as long ago as in the mid-4th century BC.

Since then, options have been present in different markets in one way or another, right up until the creation of the CBOE around 1973, when they were appropriately standardized for the earliest time, and trading of options gained some authority. Given below are the details of the history of trading options and options, beginning with Ancient Greece and moving right through to the present day.

Thales and the Olive Harvest

A book printed in the mid-4th century by Aristotle, a Greek

philosopher of huge influence and author of many subjects, provides the earliest recorded example of options trading. Aristotle consists of an account of another theorist, Thales of Miletus, and how he earned from an olive harvest in this book, entitled "Politics."

Thales had a great interest in mathematics and astronomy, among other things, and he merged his knowledge of those subjects to make what were the earliest known option contracts effectively. Thales predicted by studying the stars that there would be a massive olive harvest in his area and set out to benefit from his prediction. He acknowledged that there would be a major need for olive presses and intended to corner the market fundamentally.

Thales, however, did not have sufficient funds to own all the olive presses, so instead, he paid each olive press owner a sum of money to get the rights to make use of them at the time of harvest. Thales's rights were resold to olive presses by him to persons who required them and made a considerable profit when harvest time came around, and as Thales had forecast, it was indeed a huge harvest.

Though the term was not applied at the time, with olive presses as the underlying security, Thales had successfully made the first call option. He had paid for the right to make use of the olive presses at a fixed price, but not the obligation, and was then able to practice his options for revenue. This is the fundamental principle of how requests work today; we now have other variables, such as financial instruments and commodities, as the core security instead of olive presses.

Tulip Bulb Mania in the 17th Century

Another related event in the past of options was an incident in Holland in the 17th century that is commonly referred to as Tulip Bulb Mania. Tulips were very popular in that region at the time and were thought of as symbols of status among the Dutch gentry. Their fame had also spread to Europe and around the world, and this had headed to a dramatic increase in the need for tulip bulbs.

By this point in the past, calls and puts, mainly for hedging purposes, were used in various markets. Tulip growers, for example, would purchase puts to safeguard their revenues just in case the cost of tulip bulbs went down. The tulip wholesalers would then purchase calls to guard against the risk of rising tulip bulb prices. It should be noted that these agreements were not as advanced as they are today, and the markets for options were comparatively informal and entirely unregulated.

The need for tulip bulbs remained to increase during the 1630s, and the price also increased in value because of this. As a result, the cost of tulip bulb options' bonds rose, and a secondary market arose for these deals that allowed anyone to wonder on the tulip bulb market. In Holland, many people and families invested heavily in these contracts, frequently using all their money or even borrowing from resources like their property.

The cost of tulip bulbs continued to increase, but not for so long could it continue, and the bubble eventually burst. Prices had gone up to the end where they were unsustainable, and as prices began to fall, buyers began to disappear. So many of those who had put the cost of tulip bulbs at risk were totally wiped out. They lost all their wealth and their dwellings to ordinary people. The economy of the Netherlands also entered a recession.

There was no other way to push investors to meet their option contract's obligations because the options market was unregulated, and this eventually led to options earning a poor reputation worldwide.

Bans on Options Trading

Options still held an appeal for many investors, regardless of the bad name that these contracts had. This was mainly because they were provided excellent leverage power, that is truly one of the grounds why today they are so common. So, the trading of these contracts resumed to take place, but their bad repute could not be dispelled. Increased disapproval of their use was also expressed.

In many parts of the world, options have been prohibited several times throughout history: mainly in Japan, Europe, and even in certain states in America. The most remarkable of the bans, perhaps, was in London, England. Opposition to them was not overcome in the late 1600s, despite the emergence of an integrated sector for calls and placements, and options were eventually made unlawful in the early 18th century.

This prohibition lasted more than a hundred years and was not raised until later in the 19th century.

Jesse Livermore's investing philosophy

The bucket shop in America in the 1920s was made famous by a man named Jesse Livermore. Options seem to have made their debut in the USA through what was described as "bucket shops." Livermore speculated on the movements in stock prices; he did not own the securities on which he was betting but merely forecast their future prices. He was a stock option bookie at the beginning of his career, taking the opposite side of anyone who thought a specific stock might rise or decrease in price. If someone came to him speculating that the stock of

XYZ Company was going to go up, he would opt for the reverse side.

The investing philosophy of Jesse Livermore was not foolproof, but he is still recognized as one of the greatest traders in history.

Russell Sage and Put & Call Brokers

A significant change in the account of options trading is associated with an American financier by the name of Russell Sage. In the late 19th century, Sage started making calls and options that might be traded in the US over the counter. There was no formal exchange market yet, but Sage generated action that was a breakthrough for the trading of options.

It is also thought that Sage is the leading person to set up a pricing relation between an option's price, the underlying security's price, and interest rates. To develop synthetic loans that were made by him through the purchasing of securities and an associated put from a client, he used the principle of put-call parity.

This made it possible for him to loan money effectively to the client at an interest amount that he could decide by fixing the contract price and the appropriate strike prices consequently. Due to significant losses, Sage ultimately ceased trading in his path, but he was instrumental in the continual evolution of the trading of options.

Dealers and Brokers began to place advertisements during the late 1800s to attract sellers and buyers of options contracts with a viewpoint to brokering contracts. The concept was that the broker would be contacted by a concerned party and show their concern in buying either puts or calls on a specific stock. On the other side of the transaction, the broker would then seek to find someone.

This was somehow a laborious procedure, and the two related parties essentially determined the terms of each contract. In order to establish systems that could help in matching sellers and buyers of contracts more efficiently, the Put and Call Brokers and Dealers Association was formed, but still, there was no baseline for rating them, and there was a noticeable lack of market liquidity.

By this point, the options trading was surely growing, although the dearth of any rule meant that shareholders were still cautious.

The Listed Options Market

Put and call brokers continued to essentially control the market for options, with deals being traded over the stall. In the market, there was some consistency, and more individuals got conscious of these agreements and their possible uses. With restricted action at this time, the market remained relatively illiquid.

The brokers made their revenues from the spread between whatever the buyers were prepared to give and what the brokers were prepared to accept, but there was no specific right price system, and it was easy for the brokers to set the spread as large as they liked.

While the Securities and Exchange Commission (SEC) in the US had introduced some regulations in the market for over the security options, by the early 1960s, their trading was not really advancing at any visible rate. Too many complications were involved, and unpredictable values had also made it very hard for any stockholder to take options seriously as a feasible tradable tool.

In 1968, it was an essentially unrelated event that eventually led to a solution that would eventually bring the market for options into the mainstream.

The Chicago Board of Trade experienced a major decline in commodity futures trading on its exchange in 1968, and the organization started to look for innovative ways to excel in its business. The objective was to expand and create further trade opportunities for exchange members. The decision was taken, after considering a few alternatives, to establish a formal exchange for the exchange of options contracts.

For this to become possible, there were several barriers to overcome, but the Chicago Board of Options Exchange (CBOE) started trading in 1973. Options deals were adequately standardized for the first time, and there was a good market for them to be operated. At the same time, for centralized clearing and ensuring the appropriate completion of contracts, the Options Clearing Corporation was created. Finally, it was more than 2,000 years after the first call was made by Thales. That finally led to the legitimacy of options trading.

Evolution of Options Trading

There were very few contracts listed when the CBOE opened for trading, and they were just calling because, at this point, puts were not standardized. The idea of trading options was also still somewhat opposed, largely due to problems in verifying whether they presented a good amount for money.

The absence of a clear method for analyzing a fair option price, blended with widespread, required that there was still a lack of liquidity in the market. Another important growth helped to alter that in a little time after the opening of the CBOE for trading.

Two professors, Myron Scholes and Fisher Black designed a mathematical formula in that same year of 1973. The formula was good enough to compute the Options price by using standardized variables. As investors began to feel more comfortable trading options, this formulation became known as the Black Scholes Pricing Model, and it had a great impact.

The daily volume of agreements traded on the CBOE was above 20,000 by 1974, and two more trading floors of options were opened in America in 1975. The sum of stocks on which options could be exchanged was risen in 1977, and puts on the exchanges were also launched. More option trades were formed around the globe in the following years, and the variety of contracts that could be exchanged continued to develop.

Online trading began to gain popularity near the end of the 20th century, which made the trading of various financial tools far more accessible to participants of the public across the world. With a huge number of professional and amateur traders, the quality and quantity of the electronic brokers accessible on the web expanded, and electronic options trading became famous.

There are hundreds of contracts that are being listed on the trades in the modern options market, and millions of contracts trade every day. Trading in options continues to increase in fame and reveals no signs of reducing.

The regulatory framework for Options

In the beginning, rampant illegal activities plagued the commodity futures markets and stock options markets. Today, the most traded options are on the Chicago Board of Options Exchange (CBOE). Like stock markets, the activities of options markets draw a great deal of scrutiny from regulatory agencies such as the SEC and, in some cases, from the FBI. The market for commodities today is also tightly controlled. The Commodity Exchange Act prohibits the illegal trading of futures contracts and, through the Commodity Futures Trading Commission, mandates the particular procedures required in the industry. A variety of problems concern regulatory agencies, many of which stem from the highly computerized nature of today's trading environment. In order to create an "even" playing field for all investors, price-fixing and collusion are still problems that the agencies try to prohibit.

Bottom line

In scope and sophistication, today's futures markets vary greatly from the barter schemes that were first set up by the Japanese. Advances in technology have produced trading options and futures readily available to the average investor, as you might suspect. Most options and futures are electronically executed and go through the Options Clearing Corporation

(OCC), a clearing agency. Their global reach is another aspect of today's options and futures markets. Most big states have futures markets and exchanges of futures on products ranging from weather, commodities, stocks, and now even returns from Hollywood films. The futures market has global breadth, the same as the stock market. It is not without consequence to globalize futures exchanges. Fundamentals and psychology of the market went down with incredible intensity, as we saw during the meltdowns of the last decade, mainly due to product securities. The results for the stock and futures markets might have been too worse had there been no government intervention.

CHAPTER 2: Learn about Options and Basics of Options Trading

Options are securities that grant the investor the option to purchase or sell an asset at a predetermined price, called the strike price, over a specified period of time, without any specific precondition. The amount of time may be as brief as a day, or as lengthy as a few years, depending on the form of contract available. There are only two forms of regular contracts with options: a call and a put.

Trading options is simple to understand, as long as you learn certain important points. Investor portfolios are generally built with multiple asset classes. These could include stocks, bonds, ETFs and even mutual funds. Options are another asset class and offer many advantages that trading stocks and ETFs alone cannot possibly offer when used correctly.

2.1 Salient Features of Options

Like other asset classes, options can be purchased with an investment account. Options are strong because they can improve the portfolio of an individual. They do this by adding income, providing safeguards and even leverage. Depending, there is typically a scenario of options tailored to the target of an investor. To limit downside losses, a common example would be to use options as an efficient hedge against a decreasing stock market. Also, options can be used to produce recurring profits. In addition, they are commonly used for gambling reasons, such as wagering on stock direction. Trading of options involves certain risks that the investor must be aware of before making a trade. Options involve risks and are not appropriate for everyone. Trading of options may be risky in nature and bear a significant risk of failure.

• An option is a contract that gives the buyer the right, but not the obligation, to buy or sell (in the case of a call) the underlying asset at a specific price on or before a specific date.

• Traders use income, speculation and risk-hedging options.

• Options are also referred to as derivatives since they derive their value from the underlying assets.

• A stock option contract usually comprises 100 percent of the underlying stock, but options can be drawn upon some type of underlying properties, from debt to currency to product.

Customization is all about trading with options. Rewards may be big, but so can the danger, so there's plenty to choose from. But it's not easy to get started, and there is potential for pricey errors.

2.2 Types of Options

There are two options. It is important to note; the owner is not obliged to exercise his or her right to buy or sell for both types of options contracts. A brief description and roles of each are given below:

Call Option

A call option contract grants the owner the right to purchase 100 shares of specified security within a specified time frame at a specified price. A call option provides you the right to buy a stock at a certain price by a specific date, with the expiration option. The call buyer will give a sum of cash called a premium for this right, which the call supplier will get. Not Like stocks that can live in perpetuity, after expiration, an option will stop to exist, ending either worthlessly or with some worth.

Components of Call Option

The following elements contain the major characteristics of an option:

Strike price

At this price, you will purchase the underlying stock

Premium

The cost of the option, for the buyer or the seller

Expiration

It is when the option runs out and is settle down

How does a Call Option Work

Each option is considered a deal, and the underlying stock contains 100 securities in each deal. Exchanges quote options in terms of interest per unit, not the overall amount you have to pay to buy the deal. For example, on the exchange, an option might be estimated at $0.75. And it would cost (100 shares * 1 contract * $0.75), or $75 to purchase one contract.

If the purchase price is over the strike price at maturity, the call options are in the bank. The call owner may practice the option, putting up cash at the strike price to buy the stock. Or the possessor can actually sell the right to another buyer at its reasonable market price.

A call owner gains on less than the distinction between the strike price and the stock price when the premium is paid. Suppose, for starters, that a dealer purchased a $0.50 call with a $20 strike price, and that supply is $23. The option valued at $3 and the trader made revenue of 2.50 dollars.

If the purchase price at maturity falls below the selling amount, otherwise the call is out of the market and expires. The call seller retains the option for any premium obtained.

Put Option

A put option contract gives the owner the right to sell within a given time frame 100 shares of a specified security at a specified price. Each contract represents 100 shares or the stock on which the option is based. Putting options enables traders to magnify downward market changes, transforming a slight price decline into a big benefit for the put buyer.

Components of Put Option

The following components contain the major characteristics of an option:

Strike price

The price at which you will sell the underlying stock

Premium

The cost of the option, for either the buyer or the seller

Expiration

When the option runs out and is settled

How does a Put Option Work

For that privilege, the put buyer pays the put seller a premium per share. At expiry, if the price of the stock is lower than the price of the strike, the put value grows in money. The interest of the put, in this case, is proportional to the strike price minus the selling price times 100, as each contract contains 100 securities. Unless the price of the stock is greater than the strike, the put is useless.

Options as Derivatives

The options belong to the broader financial community, known as derivatives. The price of a derivative depends on or is derived from the price of something else. A stock choice is equity derivative. Options are financial securities derivatives-their value depends on some other asset's price

Buying and Selling Calls/Puts

There are four things you could do with options:

• Purchase Calls

• Sell calls

• Buy puts

• Sell puts

Buying stock provides a long position for you. Buying a call option will give you a potentially long position in the underlying stock. Short selling of stock provides you with a short position. Selling a naked or uncovered call in the underlying stock gives you a potential short position.

Buying a put option in the underlying stock gives you a

potentially short position. Selling a put option gives you a theoretically long place in the stock underlying it.

Those who purchase options are classified as investors, and others who offer options are named options writers. Here's the big difference between holders and writers:

There is no requirement for call investors and put investors (buyers) to buy or sell. They are granted the opportunity to exercise their privileges. This reduces the chance of options owners to just paying the premium.

However, call writers and put writers (sellers) are obliged to buy or sell if the option expires. This means a seller may need to make good on a purchase or sell pledge. It also means that sellers of options are subject to additional and, in certain situations, infinite threats. It ensures writers will risk a lot more than the quality of premium options.

Options Expiration & Liquidity

Also, options can be categorized according to their duration. Short-term options are options which usually terminate within one year. Long-term options with expirations longer than one year are known as shares where the holder hopes for a jump in price in the long-term. LEAPS are similar to standard solutions; they simply last longer.

Also, options can be distinguished when their expiry date falls. Sets of options also regularly expire on a Monday, at month's end, or even hourly. Index and ETF choices also often sell expiries annually.

American and European Options

American options can be exercised at any period between the acquisition date and the expiry date. European alternatives vary from American choices in that they should only be used on the termination day at the close of their expiry time. The difference between American and European options has nothing to do with geography. Many equity indexing options are European-style. Since the right to exercise early has some value, an American option typically carries a premium higher than a European option, which is otherwise identical. This is because the feature of early exercise is desirable and commands a premium.

Speculation

A speculator might think a stock's price will rise on the basis of fundamental analysis or technical analysis. A speculator may purchase stock or purchase a call on the stock option. Speculating with an incentive to call — rather than purchasing the stock directly — is appealing to certain traders because options have leverage. An out-of-the-money call option will pay just a few bucks, or just cents, relative to a $100 full stock price.

Hedging

Hedging with options is intended to reduce risk at a reasonable expense. Say you intend to buy inventories of equipment. Yet you do want losses to be minimal. You will reduce the downside exposure by utilizing put options and reap all the upside in a cost-effective manner. Call options may be used by short sellers to reduce losses if incorrect-particularly during a short squeeze.

2.3 Advantages of Options Trading

Options provide more planned (and economic) leeway to investors than they can get by selling, buying or shorting stocks. Traders can use portfolio loss protection options, snag security for less than it manages to sell on the open marketplace (or offer it for more), maximize the total returns on a current or new position, and reduce the risk of speculative betting under all kinds of market situations.

Yes, in the pros vs. cons of options trading, there are a lot of positives. But there are inherent risks as well. Here are some things that should be considered by every prospective options trader.

It requires a lower financial commitment as compared to stock trading

The cost of purchasing an option (the premium along with the trading commission) is much lower than what a trader would have to pay to buy shares directly.

Traders pay less money to play in the same sandbox, but they will gain just as much (percentage - wise) if the trade goes their way as the trader who shelled out for the stock.

There's the limited downside for buyers of options

You are not required to follow through on the trade when you purchase a put or call option. If your assumptions are incorrect about the time frame and direction of the trajectory of stock, your losses are limited to anything you paid for the contract as well as trading fees. For options sellers, however, the downside can be much higher.

Options offer built-in flexibility for traders

Before the expiry of an options contract, investors have the liberty to use various strategic moves, including:

- Use the option and purchase the shares to add to their portfolio

- Use the option, purchase the shares and then sell some or all of them

- Sell the "in the money" options contract to a different investor

- Has the option to recover some of the money incurred on an "out of the money" option. This can be done by selling the contract to another investor before its expiry

Options enable an investor to fix a stock price

Options contracts allow investors to freeze the stock price at a specific amount of dollars (the strike price) for a specific period of time in an action similar to putting something on layaway. Based on the type of option used, it ensures that investors will be able to purchase the stock at the strike price any time before the expiry of the option contract.

2.4 Drawbacks of Options Trading

Given below are some of the disadvantages of options trading that must be taken into consideration, especially by a beginner.

Options expose sellers to extreme losses

Contrary to an option buyer (or holder), -losses of much greater value- than the price of the contract- can be incurred by the option seller (writer). Remember, when an investor opts to write a put or call at a predetermined price, he or she is required to purchase or sell shares within the time frame irrespective of the fact whether the price is in his favor or against.

Options are time-specific

Short term is the basic essence of options. Investors of options are seeking to benefit from a near-term market change that could take place for the trade/contract to generate pay off within days, weeks or months. This requires two correct decisions to be made: determining the best time to obtain the option contract and determining specifically whether to exercise, sell or step away before the offer expires. There isn't a deadline for long-term equity buyers. They have time to let their investment play out for years, even decades.

Pre-requisites for potential traders

You must apply for clearance from your broker before even starting trading options. The broker may grant you a trading class that determines what kinds of options trades you are permitted to place after addressing a number of questions regarding your financial capital, investing background and your knowledge on the inherent risks of trading options. Any trader who is into options' trading must hold in their trading account a minimum of $2,000, which is an industry-standard and a cost of investment worth contemplating.

Options' trading involves additional costs

Any trading strategy for options (such as selling call options on stocks you don't actually own) enables buyers to set up a margin account, which is simply a line of credit that acts as collateral in the event that the transaction shifts against the investor. For the opening of a margin account, each brokerage company has various minimum conditions and may base the sum and interest rate on how much cash and shares are in the account. Usually, margin loan interest rates may range between the low single digits and the low double digits.

If an investor is unwilling to make good on loan (or if the value of the trading account falls below a certain amount, which may happen due to regular market fluctuations), if he or she does not add more cash or securities to it, the lender may trigger a margin call and liquidate an investor's portfolio.

The Options Clearing Corporation offers a comprehensive overview of the features and risks of standardized options and an overview of the U.S. federal income tax rules that impact those looking to invest in options and other financial products.

Bottom line

You must recognize the company's market inside out and determine whether to purchase, sell or retain stock for the long term and have a good understanding of the way the asset is going. Investors of options ought to be hyper-aware of those items and more.

Success in options demands from investors to have a clear idea of the inherent value of the firm, but perhaps most significantly, they will need to have a sound thesis of how the business has been and would be impacted by short-term variables such as internal activities, sector/competition, and macroeconomic impacts.

Many investors can conclude that options offer their financial lives with excessive uncertainty. But the options trading strategies for beginners can help limit your downside if you are interested in exploring the possibilities that options offer and have the right discipline and the capital to endure potential losses.

2.5 Basics of Options' Pricing

The value of stock options is determined from their underlying shares' value and, depending on the results of the associated shares, the trading price for options can increase or decrease. With options, there are a variety of elements to understand.

The Strike Price

The strike price for an option is the rate at which, if the option is exercised, the underlying asset is purchased or sold. In the peculiar jargon of options, the relationship between the strike price and a stock's market price determines the following:

- Option is in-the-money
- Options are at-the-money
- Option is out-of-the-money

In-the-money

The strike price of an in-the-money call option is below the real market price. Example: At the $95 strike price for WXYZ, an investor buys a call option that is already trading at $100. The investor's position is $5 in-the-money. The call option grants the investor the right to purchase the shares at $95. The strike price of an In-the-Money Put option is above the real market price. Example: At the WXYZ's $110 strike price, which is currently trading at $100, an investor buys a Put option. In-the-money is $10 for this investor position. The Put option grants the seller the right to sell equity at $110.

At the money

For both Put and Call options, the strike and the actual stock prices are the same.

Out-of-the-money

The strike price of an out-of-the-money call option is above the real market price. Example: At the strike price of $120 for ABCD, which is actually trading at $105, an investor buys an out-of-the-money call option. The position of this investor is $15 out-of-the-money. The strike price of an out-of-the-money put option is below the real market price. Example: At the $90 strike price of ABCD, which is currently priced at $105, an investor buys an out-of-the-money Put option. The position of that investor is $15 out-of-the-money.

The Premium

The premium is the price for an option that a customer pays to the seller. On purchasing, the premium is paid upfront and is not reimbursable-even though the option is not applied. Premiums on a per-share base are quoted. So, a $0.21 premium reflects a $21.00 per option contract ($0.21 x 100 shares) premium payment. There are many considerations that decide the amount of the premium-the prevailing stock price in comparison to the strike price (intrinsic value), the period of time before the offer expires (time value) and the price fluctuations of the commodity (volatility value).

Intrinsic value + Value of time + Value of volatility = option price

For example, at a strike price of $80, an investor buys a three-month call option for volatile security that trades at $90.

Intrinsic Value = $10

Time value = because the call is 90 days away, the time value will be slightly applied to the price.

Volatility value = Because the underlying security is volatile, the volatility premium might be added.

Factors that influence options prices

The following factors have an impact on options prices:

- The underlying equity price in relation to the strike price (intrinsic value)

- The length of time until the option expires (time value)

- How much the price fluctuates (volatility value)

Ancillary factors that influence option prices

- Additional facts that have an impact on options prices are:

- The underlying equity's quality

- The underlying equity's dividend rate

- Prevailing market conditions

- The underlying equity's supply and demand for options

- The existing interest rates

Additional costs: Taxes and commissions

Investors that trade options, as in virtually any investment, must pay income taxes and also commissions to brokers on options trades. The net profit gain would be impacted by these costs.

2.6 Pricing Spreads in Options and Trading Strategies

A call spread relates to the purchasing of a call on a strike, and the selling of another call for a higher strike of the same expiry. An option strategy in which a call option is purchased is a call spread, and another less costly call option is sold.

A put spread relates to purchasing a put on strike and selling another put on the same expiry's lower price. An option technique in which a put option is purchased is a put spread, and another less costly put option is sold.

This transaction is less dangerous than an outright buy since the call and put options have identical features, but it often provides less benefit. If you think that the underlying price will shift in a certain direction, and wish to reduce your original outlay if the forecast is wrong, these techniques are beneficial to try.

Advantages of Spreads

When you want to mitigate risk, spreads are useful for trading. Typically, spreads are traded by arbitragers to gain an edge on the transaction with close strikes and then control the position. The position takes in trading premiums as the short option premium tends to cover the cost of the long option.

Call spreads buying considerations

Consider buying call spreads in the following situations:

If you are sure that the underlying security is destined to go up after which volatility will subside (e.g., a news event)

When you are sure that the underlying security is definitely going to edge up moderately

When you are sure that the underlying security's price will decline sharply, thus generating a sale of the underlying security

Consequently, the call spread will guard you against a petty upside move

Put spreads buying considerations

Consider buying put spreads in the following situations:

If you are sure that the underlying security is going to edge downward, resulting in a decrease in volatility (e.g., a news event)

If you are sure that the underlying security is going to depict a decline in a limited range

If you are sure that the underlying security is going to fall sharply

Bull call spread

One long call, along with a lower strike price plus one short call at a higher strike price, is a bull call spread. The very underlying stock and the same expiry period are required for both calls. For a net debit (or net cost) and gains as the underlying stock increases in price, a bull call spread is built. Profit is impaired if the stock price rises above the short call strike price, and the possible loss is restricted if the stock price moves below the long call strike price (lower risk).

Bear Call Spread

A bear call spread, or bear call credit spread, is a form of the strategy of options that are used when an options trader assumes the cost of the main stock to fall. By buying call options at a particular strike price while selling the same amount of calls at the same maturity date, but at a shorter strike price, a bear call spread is established. Using this technique, the utmost profit to be made is equivalent to the credit earned while starting the trade.

A short call spread is another name for a bear call spread. It is deemed as a strategy with limited-risk and limited-reward.

Calendar call spreads

You sell and purchase a call with the same strike price while running a calendar spread with calls, but the call you purchase would have a later date of expiry than the call you sell. As expiration approaches, you take advantage of accelerating time decay on the front-month call, also known as a shorter-term call. You want to purchase back the shorter-term call right before the front-month expiration for almost nothing. You will sell the back-month call and close your position at the same moment. Ideally, there would also be considerable time value for the back-month call.

Create your calendar spread with at-the-money calls if you're expecting limited price change. Use marginally out-of-the-money calls if you're moderately bullish. This will help you with lower up-front costs.

Bear Put Spread

A bear put spread consists of a higher strike price for one long put and a lower strike price for one short put. Both puts have the same underlying stock and the same expiry date. For a net debit (or net cost) and earnings as the underlying stock decreases in price, a bear put spread is created. Profit is restricted if the stock price falls below the lower strike price of the short put strike), and if the stock price rises above the longput strike price (higher strike), the possible loss is limited.

Bull Put spread

A bull put spread consists of a higher strike price for a short put and a lower strike price for a long put. Both puts have the same underlying security and the same expiry date. For a net credit (or net sum received) and gains from either an increasing equity price or from time erosion or from both, a bull put spread is created. A potential benefit is restricted to the net premium earned fewer commissions, and potential loss is reduced if the stock price drops below the longput strike price.

Calendar put spread

By purchasing one "longer-term" put and selling one "shorter-term" put with the same strike price, a long calendar spread with puts is established. Consider the following example. 100 Put is bought for two months (56 days to expiration), and 100 Put is sold for one month (28 days to expiration). For a net debt (net cost), this strategy is established, and both the profit

---

opportunity and the risk are minimal. If the stock price matches the strike price of the puts on the closing date of the short put, the maximum profit is obtained, and the maximum risk is achieved if the stock price shifts sharply away from the strike price.

2.7 Buying a Call Option

The buyer of an option call search to generate revenue if and when the price of the underlying profit rises to a price higher than the strike price of the option. On the other hand, the call option seller expects the asset's price will fall, or at least never raise as much as the strike/exercise price value until it ends, in which case the money earned for selling the choice would be pure income. If the price of the fundamental safety does not rise above the strike price before expiry, then the option will not be cost-effective for the purchaser to exercise the option, and the option will end valueless or "out of the money." The buyer experiences a loss equivalent to the cost given for the call option. Otherwise, if the cost of the fundamental protection falls past the strike price, the investor may exercise this choice profitably.

For example, imagine you've purchased an option on 100 stocks, with a $30 option to hit before your option runs out; the stock price increases from $28 - $40. You will then exercise the right to purchase 100 stock options at $30, granting you an instant $10 a shared benefit. Your overall income will be 100 options, $10 for a share, minus the sales price you were charged for the option. If you had paid $200 for the call option in this case, then your net income will be $800 (100 shares x $10 per share-$ 200 = $800).

Buying call options helps buyers to spend a small sum of money to theoretically gain from a price increase in the basic safety, or to guard against the positional risks.

Swing traders can use options to transform small quantities of money into large profits, while business and institutional shareholders make use of options to boost their marginal profits.

2.8 Selling a Call Option

Sellers of call options, called writers, offer call options in the expectation that they may become useless by the expiration date. They earn money by pocketing the rates (prices) they have been paying. An income will be lowered, or possibly turn into a net loss if the option holder performs the option profitably as the fundamental safety price falls past the option strike point. The call options are offered in two ways:

Covered Call Option

If the call option seller owns the underlying stock, then a call option is covered. Selling the call options on these fundamental securities brings in extra gain, which would mitigate any anticipated market price decreases. The seller option is "covered" against failure since, in the event that the buyer option exercises its option, the seller can give the buyer with stock shares, which he has already bought at a cost below the option's strike price. The seller's income is holding the underlying stock would be restricted to raising the stock to the strike price, but he will be shielded from any real loss.

Naked Call Option

If a trader of options offers a call option without buying the underlying stock, a naked call option is provided. Naked short-selling options are Known as dangerous when there is no cap on how big a stock's price can go, and the seller of the option is not "covered" by keeping the underlying stock against potential losses. When a call option investor uses his or her privilege, the naked option seller is obliged to acquire the stock at the existing market price to supply the option owner with the securities. If the stock price surpasses the strike price of the call option, then the change between the current market price and the strike price signifies the seller's loss. Most option sellers command a high cost to offset any possible losses.

2.9 Selling and Buying a Put Option

You can produce double-digit income and gains by selling put options even in a smooth, bearish or overrated market. For big returns on investment, you don't need a strong market or speedy business growth. In the case of a market collapse, you may even grant your investments a 10 percent guarantee against the downside. In other words, if the market falls by 25%, your equity locations are likely to fall by only 15%. You can also enter stock positions exactly at the cost you need and keep the cost base low. You should try to purchase in a declining market to get a greater bargain instead of buying at presently available market rates. Like any device, there is a perfect period and place for selling put options, and at certain times, it is not an optimal strategy. This is a sophisticated and best way of entering equity positions when used correctly.

To option sellers, the two most critical things are the strike and the bid. The strike is the amount you agree to buy the shares for if the option is exercised, and the bid is about the amount you can expect to earn on selling the option. If you sell an option with a strike price of $30 below the current stock price of $30.50, you will now receive $143 from the option buyer, and you will be obliged to purchase 100 shares of the company at $30 each if the buyer wishes, for a total of $3,000, at any time before the option expires in 3.5 months.

If the particular company's stock generally stays above $30 / share over the next 3.5 months, the option buyer probably won't assign the shares to you, as there would be no reason for her to force you to pay exactly $30 / share when the market price is already above $30 / share. Her option will expire worthlessly, you will keep your $143 premium, and your $3,000 in secured cash will be released for another option to be sold. Here is the calculated rate of return, if the right expires: $143 / $2,857 = 0.05 = 5%

After around 3.5 months, you made a return yield of 5 percent on your initial currency. This will be around 18 percent annualized returns on your investment if you practice that for the remainder of the year a few times. Compare this with the historical return of the S&P 500 of around 9%. Compared to average stock returns, you're being charged a huge amount of money to only hang around and wait for a market drop on a business you'd like to buy. On the contrary, if the stock dips to $29.50 / share, you still have to retain the $143 premium, and

the buyer option will assign you to purchase the 100 shares for $30 each.

This means that your effective cost base for buying those shares was only $28.57, which, as you wanted, is below your target buy price. You ended up having to purchase them for $30 apiece, but you still got a $1.43 / share bonus upfront, which covered some of the expenses. The total cost structure is that for 100 securities, you have to spend $28.57 / share, or $2.857. So instead, you hold 100 shares of a company already selling for $29.50 each. You purchased a wonderful business at a decent price, and ideally, you should still anticipate lots of growth in profits and dividends over time.

2.10 Collars

A collar option technique, also known as a hedge wrapper or just collar, is an options strategy used to minimize an underlying asset's both positive and negative returns. It restricts the return of the portfolio to a defined range and may hedge the position against the underlying asset's potential volatility. The use of a protective put and covered call option produces a collar position. It is produced more precisely by keeping an underlying stock, purchasing an option that is out of the money, and selling an option that is out of the money call.

The method-Creating a Collar Position

The collar position is created by using the following method:

Collar Position=Long Underlying Asset + Long Put Option + Short Call Option

2.11 Combinations

A combination is a type of an options trading strategy that entails both purchasing and selling of call and put options on the same underlying stock.

Call & Put Buying Combinations

Following are the call and put buying combinations:

Straddle

The straddle is an infinite profit, low-risk options trading technique that is utilized anytime the trader in options expects that the underlying asset price can make a big shift in the price in the immediate future in any direction. By purchasing an equivalent sum of at-the-money call and put options of the same expiration date, it can be established.

Strangle

Strangle is also a technique of limited risk and infinite profit potential, like the straddle. The distinction between the two tactics is that out-of-the-money options are bought to build the strangle, minimizing the cost of maintaining the position, while at the same time needing a significantly greater change in the price of the underlying to be lucrative for the strategy.

CHAPTER 3: Getting ready to Start Options Trading

If you're thinking about trading options for generating profits, you may wonder if it's a decent time to start trading. Guidelines are available that you could always follow.

Get out of Debt

Get out of debt first. Pay off the car loans and credit card balances, explicitly. It's because of those loans; you're losing income anyway.

Instances of' good debt' are known to be leases and student loans, while auto loans and credit card balances are perceived as instances of' bad debt.'

The bottom line is that, before you start trading options, you must get out of bad debt.

Don't Learn the Hard Way

You're also not fully in a spot to trade options even after you've eliminated the bad debt. You first have to know yourself. And if you believe you're ready and in the past you traded stocks; you still aren't done.

Trading options are totally separate from trading securities. And before you trade options, you have to understand the stock market; however, you still need to learn quite a bit more. Start by studying the essentials. Understand the distinction between options for calls and options for put. Know about expiration dates for contracts and strike prices.

The trading of options is for persons who delve extensively into the data to assess the most advantageous trades. Traders who overlook certain stats are sometimes burnt. When you've mastered the basics, it's time to learn about various options strategies.

- Spreads

- Straddles

- Strangles

- Iron butterflies

- Iron condors

- Never Stop Learning

  When it applies to options trading, you have never "arrived." There is always something that an expert trader will learn from you. Keep practicing also though you have trained yourself and mastered trading to the extent that you value your expertise as a trader. Strive to make yourself a greater trader every day.

Practice Makes Perfect

Before you allocate real capital, you need to do some practice trading. This is because, before doing the real thing, everybody wants to do some practice trading.

When you invest in the capital markets, there are things you can learn. The quick way rather than the rough way is easier to learn such lessons.

Fortunately, trading platforms are accessible that enable you to learn to trade. Without losing some of your hard-earned assets, you can establish a pretend portfolio and begin trading stocks and options. And, as time progresses, you will see how the trades are successful. Take the time to assess what went wrong if you're not profitable so that you can stop making such errors in the future.

3.1 Educate yourself on requirements for opening an Options trading account

Stock market options are limited-term contracts that offer owners the right to purchase or sell particular securities at a fixed date. In a broad variety of market techniques, the two forms of options — puts and calls — may be used to benefit from potential shifts in equity prices. To start purchasing and selling puts and calls, you must first register for account authorization.

A trading account for options is a cash, margin or IRA stock brokerage account to which trading authorization for options has been applied. By completing a separate document, you incorporate options permission, plus a declaration of your trading background. The regulatory department of the broker checks the application for options and accepts your account with a degree of trading permission varying from one to five. What options strategies may be traded in the account are decided by the authorization levels. Novice investors can obtain one or two levels of authorization that enable strategies for lower-risk options.

3.2 Learn on how to read and execute options contracts

Option contracts are purchased and sold using the online investment account's options trading screen. Under the options-chain link of a given stock, various put and call option choices can be identified. Choosing an option from the chain fills the trading screen with the specifics of a single option. You may then decide how many contracts you choose to purchase or sell and, if necessary, set a cap price. For a market order, the currently quoted "bid" price of an option is what you will pay to purchase. If you sell on the market, the "bid" price is what you would get. Each option contract is on an underlying stock of 100 securities, so one contract costs 100 times the quoted amount.

3.3 Get informed on open and close orders

To start a trading position, options may be either bought or sold. Buying options grants you the right to purchase (call options) and/or sell (put options) the actual stock securities at a particular amount. If the customer uses his privileges under the options you have sold, trading options add option premium earnings to the portfolio and the obligation to sell or purchase stock. You execute a buy-to-open or sell-to-open order to open an options position, depending on your approach. The order would be a sell-to-close or buy-to-close to close an options position in your portfolio.

3.4 Look for the minimum amount required to trade options

To trade options, each online broker needs a different minimum balance. The mandatory minimum deposit for most brokerages is less than $1,000. Investors fill out a brief questionnaire inside their investment account to submit for options trading authorization. It is possible to get access to begin executing options directly afterward.

Options Trading Platforms

To an online broker, there is no consumer more important than an options investor. Trades of options give brokers far larger operating profits than equity trades, and competitiveness is fierce for attracting these consumers as a consequence. This sort of business environment is perfect for consumers because product creativity and efficient prices come with fair competition. One can check for the following important characteristics when choosing a trading platform:

Speed

It should be a web-based platform with the ability to deliver speed, ensuring ease of use, and the tools needed for traders to succeed.

Low costs

Commissions and other charges should be a matter of concern as these are deducted from your profits.

Options tools

The desktop application should have easy trading and intensive analysis. Option software should have a personalized classification, real-time Greek streaming, and specialized position analysis for existing positions.

It must give and show all the resources that an options trader would like in an efficient way. Some of them could be spread groupings, easy strategy screening, and risk/reward details that are simple to grasp. It must encourage customers to build custom rules and instantly roll up their current options positions. It should be outstanding for the number of settings and depth of choice.

Trading platforms can be built for both novice and experienced options traders. You, as an investor, should expect from your broker to include scanning, P&L analysis, risk analysis, and easy-order management.

3.5 The Broker

Trading profitably allows you to use a brokerage company that aligns with your financial priorities, educational requirements and personal style.

Choosing the right online stockbroker that suits your needs, particularly for new investors, may mean the difference between an exciting new income stream and crushing disappointment.

Although there are no surefire means of guaranteeing returns on investment, a way to ensure your success is met by the selection of the online brokerage that better fits the needs of yours.

Exposure to the capital markets is simple and cheap due to a number of brokers operating online portals. Different online brokers are tailored for a particular category of the customer – from long-term buy-and-hold novices to professional, successful day traders.

Finding the right broker online needs some due diligence to get the best out of your funds. Follow the measures and guidance to pick the right one:

- Know Your Needs

- Narrow the Field

- Look at Brokerage Account Offerings

- Figure Out the Fees

- Know about Online Security and Account Protection

- Trading Commissions

- Test the Broker's Platform

- Provision of Charting Features

- Stock Broker's Quality and Usability

- How Well Does the Stock Broker Educate Its Clients

- Analytical Resources offered by the broker

- Ease of Depositing and Withdrawing Funds

- Customer Service

Margins

In options dealing, "margin" often applies to the cash or assets needed to be deposited with the brokerage company by an option writer as collateral for the obligation of the writer to purchase or sell the underlying security or, in the case of cash-settled options, to compensate the balance of the cash payout if the option is assigned.

For option writers, margin specifications are difficult and not the same for each form of the underlying security. They are subject to change and can differ from one brokerage company to another brokerage company. As they have a major effect on each trade's risk/reward profiles, option writers (whether they be calls or puts alone or as part of several position strategies like spreads, straddles or strangles) can decide the specific margin criteria of their brokerage companies and ensure that if the market turns against them, they are willing to fulfill those specifications.

Margin Requirements Manual

A margins requirements manual for various options strategies has been published by **CBOE**.

Margin Calculator

CBOE has also provided a **useful online tool** that helps to calculate the exact margin requirements for a specific trade.

Margin call

In the case of an unfavorable market movement, margins are needed to guarantee that you will fulfill your future obligations. Margins are payable for option writers only, while buyers of options do not.

An Options margin call is where the broker needs extra cash or stocks to be given by a customer who has written Options. A failure to fulfill a margin call can result in the closing of your Options positions.

How are Margins triggered

A margin call can be triggered for a score of factors, but the most common reasons are:

When a position moves against you, it consequently increases your potential obligation under the Options contract.

The exchange increases the margin requirement against your

positions. The exchange reduces the collateral value allowed on your shares deposited as cover.

CHAPTER 4: Financial Leverage and Risk Management

One of the greatest advantages of trading options is financial leverage. In order to increase profits, flexibility is generated by having your assets function harder for you. Leveraging allows a limited volume of money to build the opportunity for greater profits.

To increase potential earnings, financial leverage is typically generated by utilizing the resources of other people. In order to invest in real estate, deposits are used, and firms raise capital to increase activities. The gain of the leverage arises from the improved valuation of the land or the higher income of the business, which enhances the worth of the securities of the stockholders.

However, buying options offers intrinsic financial leverage to the user. Without the need to use borrowed money, you will control the greater amount of shares with the same initial capital by trading in options than if you owned the shares yourself.

Leverage.

For instance, you might buy 10 IMAX stock shares (hypothetically) priced at $100 per share if you choose to invest $1000. Alternatively, with lots of 100 securities ($2.00 per option), the options contracts could reasonably be priced at $200. You may acquire five options contracts for your commitment of $1 000, increasing your financial leverage by enabling you to own 500 securities instead of only 10.

If the value of such securities improves significantly throughout the option contract, you will wish to purchase the securities that you have the right to purchase at the negotiated price (strike price), which is far cheaper than the market value at that time. If you purchased the ten securities with the $1 000, you would then resell those securities at market value, making a return from a significantly higher amount of shares than the ones you might have owned initially. Obviously, though, you will need to have access to even more money to conduct this transaction in order to buy the securities that your options allow you to buy, and be able to bear the chance of unexpected decline in the stock price until you have the ability to resell your assets.

In this investment, though, the strongest source of financial leverage derives from the assumption that the percentage improvement in the option is proportionately greater than the increase in the underlying share. In order to purchase and sell the securities that your options offer you the ability to own, this leverage often comes without the expense of spending even larger sums of cash.

Let's assume in the previously stated hypothetical transaction that the value of the stock grows from $100 per and reaches $105 per share. The return that this will produce on your $1 000 expenditure would be $50, or a 5 percent raise if you purchased those 10 securities.

A fair calculation, on the other side, is that an improvement from $2.00 to $2.80 per option is the equivalent of the options you might have purchased. This creates an improvement of $400, or 40 percent, for your 500 options. This far higher possible rise is a way that leverage can easily generate by trading options.

However, it is necessary to be mindful that the prospective loss is often greater. A 5% valuation loss on stock may imply a 40 percent value loss on the corresponding options.

In trading options, knowing financial leverage, the gains and costs are very critical. Using leverage will help you to optimize your returns with an effective trading strategy while mitigating the risk.

Advantage of Leverage in Options Trading

The stability and variety they bring, and the broad variety of tactics that can be utilized, are one of the main factors that investors want to trade options. There are, in fact, a variety of methods that may be used either to minimize the danger of taking a position or to minimize the initial expense of taking a position.

It's possible to enter a trade using any of the reduced risk techniques to know precisely what the actual total loss is, which can be really helpful when organizing trades. However, trading in options is generally regarded to be high risk, and substantial losses may be incurred. Obviously, the less likely you are to have disastrous errors, the better you practice, and the more exposure you gain, but even seasoned traders will make mistakes, and it is essential to realize what form of risks you are exposed to.

The idea that you can use leverage to efficiently maximize the value of your resources is a big gain that is frequently stated. For instance, if you purchased $1,000 worth of call options based on Company X stock, then you might expect to earn even bigger money. If the stock's price increased, you must invest the $1,000 directly into the stock.

A disadvantage of Leverage in Options trading

The other side of this, though, in specific regard to the aforementioned case, is if the stock dropped in value or even only stayed the same, your call options could end up useless, and you will lose the whole $1,000. If you had purchased the stocks instead, if Business X went bankrupt, you would just lose half of the $1,000. This demonstrates a big risk, and that you might purchase options to expire worthlessly, suggesting you lose everything you have put in such contracts.

Calculating Leverage to determine how much Leverage you need

Assume that an XYZ company trading at $50 rises to $55 the next trading day. Consequently the $50 strike call options will move up from $2 to $4.50, depicting a gain of $2.50 ($5 x 0.5 = $2.50).

Therefore, the actual options leverage of an option position can be computed by using the following formula:

Options Leverage = (delta equivalent stock price - option price) / option price

Base on the above example: XYZ shares are trading at $50, and its $50 strike price call options have a delta value of 0.5:

Options Leverage = ([$50 x 0.5] - $2) / $2 = 11.5 times

The above options leverage calculation demonstrates that the $50 strike call options of XYZ company incorporate the leverage of an option of 11.5 times. This means that it gives you an opportunity to multiply your profits by 11.5 times. In other words, 11.5 times options leverage compounds your money by 11.5 times.

Options Leverage - Interpretation

In options trading, knowing multiple leverage options is important, since the higher the multiple of leverage options, the greater the chance of losing. In option investing, leverage is a double-edged weapon and risk/reward is proportionate to one another. As a result, the leverage of In The Money options will still be smaller than the leverage of At The Money Options

options and is smaller than the Out Of The Money Options.

Refer to above example where XYZ shares are trading at $50 and its

$50 strike price call options is asking for $2 with a delta value of 0.5

$45 strike price call options is asking for $6 with a delta value of 0.8

$55 strike price call options is asking for $0.10 with a delta value of 0.01

Options Leverage (1) = ([$50 x 0.5] - $2) / $2 = 11.5 times

Options Leverage (2) = ([$50 x 0.8] - $6) / $6 = 5.7 times

Options Leverage (3) = ([$50 x 0.01] - $0.01 / $0.01 = 49 times

As you can see above, the leverage of options on the out of the money $55 strike price call options is significantly greater than the leverage of options on the $45 strike price call options in the money, which also reinforces the teaching that the options that are out of the money are more risky than the options in the money.

While 49 times more benefit is given by the out of the money options, it may also cause 49 times the losses resulting in the elimination of all the capital invested if XYZ business fails to push above its strike price by expiry.

Risk & Money Management

When trading options, correctly controlling the capital and risk exposure is important. Although the risk for any sort of investment is ultimately inevitable, the risk exposure doesn't have to be an issue. The aim is to efficiently control the risk funds; please make sure you are secure with the risk amount being taken and so you are not vulnerable to excessive losses.

It is necessary to use the same principles when controlling the resources as well. Use the money that you can manage to lose while you trade; stop overstretching yourself. As efficient risk and money management is the key to effective trading of options, it is a topic that you really need to learn. Some of the strategies you may, and should, use to handle your exposure to risk and regulate your budget are listed below.

Using Your Trading Plan

A comprehensive trading strategy that sets out rules and criteria for your trading activities is really essential. Helping you control your resources, and your risk exposure is one of the realistic applications of such a plan. Your strategy should provide specifics of the risk level you are confident with and the amount of money you intend to use.

You will prevent one of the biggest mistakes that buyers and traders commit by executing the strategy by just utilizing resources that you have expressly reserved for options trading: utilizing "scared" funds.

You are much less able to make sound choices about your trade while you are investing with capital that you cannot afford to risk or could have put aside for other purposes. Although it's impossible to fully eradicate the emotion inherent with trading options, you just want to be as focused on what you do and why you do.

When emotion takes control, you can tend to lose your attention and are likely to act irrationally. For instance, it might potentially lead you to pursue losses from previous trades that had gone wrong or make purchases that you normally wouldn't do. You can have a lot greater chance at holding your feelings in check if you implement that strategy and stick to managing that financial money.

Equally, the degree of danger that you describe in your strategy should really be adhered to. If you want to make trades with low risk, so there is really no justification why you should start submitting yourself to higher risk levels. Maybe because you have created a few errors and you want to attempt to fix them, it's always enticing to do this, or perhaps you have performed better on certain low-risk transactions and want to start increasing the earnings at a quicker pace.

If you planned to make low-risk transactions, though, then you clearly did so for a reason, and because of the same emotional reasons listed above, there is no sense in putting yourself out of your comfort zone.

Managing Risk with Options Spreads

Options spreads are important and effective instruments in the trading of options. Basically, the spread of an option is where you merge more than one position on options contracts depending on the same underlying security to establish one overall trading position efficiently.

For instance, if you purchased a particular stock's in the money calls and then wrote cheaper on the same stock out of the market calls, then you might have produced a spread known as a bull call spread. If the underlying stock went up in value, purchasing the calls ensures you stand to benefit, but if the market price did not go up, you would lose any or more of the money invested in purchasing them. You will be able to manage any of the original expenses by writing calls on the same stock and thereby reduce the overall sum of money you might lose.

The usage of spreads includes many trading techniques for options, and these spreads are a very helpful way to handle risk. As with the bull call spread example provided above, you may use them to decrease the overall costs of entering a position and to reduce how much money you stand to risk. This suggests that the gains you will earn are theoretically limited, but it decreases the inherent risk.

Spreads may often be used while taking a short position to decrease the risks involved. For instance, if you wrote in the money puts on a stock, you will obtain an initial payout to write certain options, so if the stock fell in value, you will be subject to future losses. If you purchased cheaply out of the money puts as well, so you might have to expend some of the upfront investment. However, you would reduce any possible losses that might trigger a drop in the stock.

As you will see from all of these cases if the market moves in the correct direction for you, it is possible to enter positions that you also stand to prosper, yet you should narrowly restrict any losses you might suffer if the price moves against you. This is why spreads are so commonly used by traders in options; they are superb risk control instruments. There is a broad variety of spreads that can be used to benefit from nearly every market condition.

Managing Risk through Diversification

Diversification is a risk control strategy that is usually employed by investors who use a buy and hold policy to construct a portfolio of stocks. For certain buyers, the underlying concept of diversification is that the allocation of capital through various firms and industries generates a diverse portfolio rather than making so much capital locked up with one single business or industry. In general, a diversified portfolio is perceived to be less risk-exposed than a portfolio that is solely made up of one single form of investment.

Diversification is not necessary in the same manner when it comes to alternatives, but it does have its applications, and you can potentially diversify in a variety of different forms. Although the idea stays essentially the same, you don't want so much of your money allocated to a single type of investment; diversification is done across a number of strategies of options trading.

By using a variety of different tactics, by trading options depending on a number of underlying stocks, and by trading multiple forms of options, you will diversify. Essentially, the principle of utilizing diversification is that you stand to earn money in a variety of forms and with all the trades to be efficient, you are not fully dependent on one specific result.

Managing Risk Using Options Orders

Using the range of different orders that you may place is a reasonably straightforward method of handling risk. There is a range of additional instructions that you can place,

and all of these can assist you in risk control.

For instance, at the moment of implementation, a standard market order would be filled out at the best possible price. This is an absolutely common way to buy and sell options; however, the order can end up being filled at a price that is higher or lower than you expect it to be in a dynamic market. You can prevent purchasing or selling at less desirable rates by utilizing limit orders, where you can specify the minimum and maximum costs at which your order can be filled.

You may also use instructions to automate the exit of a position: whether to lock in gains already earned or to minimize losses on a deal that has not performed well. You can easily monitor at what stage you quit a position by utilizing instructions like the market stop order, the trailing stop order, or the limit stop order.

This can help you to prevent circumstances where you lose out on gains by hanging on to a position for too long or suffer major losses by not closing out rapidly enough in a terrible position.

You will restrict the risk you are subjected to each and every transaction you create by utilizing option orders accordingly.

Money Management and Position Sizing

The management of your money is inextricably related to risk management, and both are equally important. Ultimately, you have a limited amount of cash to use, and it is important to have strict management over the capital expenditure and to guarantee that you do not risk everything and that you finally become unable to do any more transactions.

Using a very basic term known as position sizing is the single best way to handle your capital. Basically, position sizing determines how much of the money you choose to use to enter some given position.

To use position sizing efficiently, in terms of a percentage of your total investment resources, you need to decide how much to spend in each specific transaction. Position sizing is a method of diversification in several respects. You would never be too focused on one particular result by just utilizing a limited percentage of your resources in any one trade. Also, the most effective traders can make transactions that rarely come out terribly; the trick is to ensure that you are not too seriously impacted by the poor ones.

For instance, if in one trade you have 50 percent of your investment resources locked up and it ends up costing you money, then you would actually have spent a large sum of your usable funds. If you prefer to only use 5 % to 10% of your money per trade, then you cannot be wiped out by even a few straight losing deals.

If you are optimistic that in the long term, your trading strategy can work, so you need to be prepared to push through the tough times and still have ample resources to turn it around. Position sizing will assist you in achieving just that.

4.1 Advanced Trading Strategies for Options

The great news is that with options, traders having all skilled levels can learn how to trade the market. Options trading techniques typically utilize momentum metrics such as the Relative Strength Index (RSI) to warn them when market moves are exaggerated, either upside-down or downside-up and are primed for a reversal in the opposing direction.

Also, traders manage to stay longer in trade. It will make them better off to operate overnight being a part of a swing trading plan, as acquired option positions have reduced downside danger.

Option traders use various options strategy, which includes buying or selling one or other options to have either market-neutral or directional views of the underlying asset market.

These often usually use diagrams called option compensation or reward profiles to provide a quick understanding of whether the option plan would payout with a variety of underlying market prices, including the one seen below, on the expiry date.

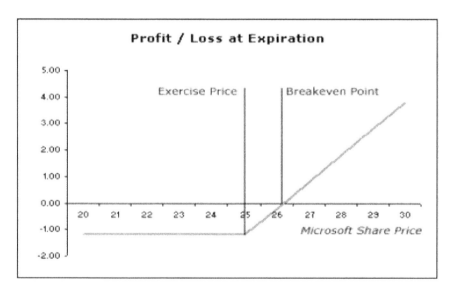

The blue line in this graph indicates how if the demand hits the breakeven stage, the option price begins making revenue at expiration. The position can also indicate a profit before expiry, however, if you can sell the option at a price higher than the purchase price. This is usually the goal when swinging trading the options.

Fortunately, you can understand how to trade options to apply your market opinion for a directional trading strategy such as swing trading. The instructions below illustrate how to use a basic option strategy to swing trade in almost every financial asset sector where options are easily accessible, such as purchasing a call or put option.

Select an Asset

The first phase in swing trading with options is to pick an underlying commodity for trade that you have established as an incentive to sell. Swing traders would also track different equity markets in order to provide a better probability of having a successful trading setup. In picking an asset, search for equity price that is prone to a downturn as defined by a measure of momentum, such as the RSI. A specific measure is a range-bound oscillator that indicates an overbought position when its cost is over 70 or oversold position when it's worth is below 30.

Look to sell a market at RSI rates over 70 and purchase it at rates below 30

When you like any more accurate swing trading indications from the RSI, you should wait before you see something occurring called price-RSI variance, which implies that the market price rises briskly, such as reaching a new peak, but the RSI does not. That's an even stronger swing trading warning that an impending recession is coming to the market.

Select a Direction

For example, If you have established demand and used your chosen method of demand research to identify a trading chance with a reasonable reward/risk ratio of two or more to one, whether technical and/or fundamental, then you may feel better utilizing call and/or put options to take a directional market view of the underlying commodity.

For e.g., if you think the demand would improve, you'd have a call option to go on the market for a long period. With restricted downside risk and limitless upside potential for the underlying market, you want to trade.

Instead, if your point of view was that the market would fall, instead, you would buy a put option, again with a restricted risk of the downside and unlimited potential for upside.

The payoff profiles shown for long call and put options at expiry shows how your losses are restricted to the premium Paid if it turns out that your directional perception is wrong. In addition, possible profits on an option position are infinite and begin to accumulate past the breakeven point where the profits on the position go beyond the bonus paid.

Call Option   Put Option

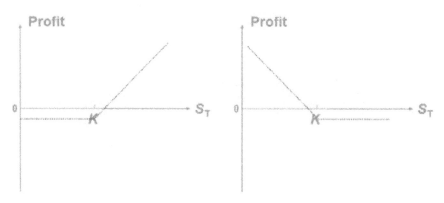

Call and put option payoff profiles with a strike price of K. Source: Surlytrader.com

Choose a Strike Price

An option's strike price aids in determining its price. The more appealing an option's strike price is in relation to the current market cost for the underlying asset, the more it will charge. Also, the longer time frame a particular strike price option has until expiry, the more it will be expensive.

When strike rates are higher than the prevalent sector, it is assumed that they are either "in the pocket." An option with an ITM strike price has "intrinsic value," corresponding to the change between the normal market price (for the delivery date of the option) and the strike price. When the strike price of an option is right on the prevailing market, it's "at the cash" or ATM, and when it is "out of cash," or OTM, at a worse level than the prevailing market. There is no inherent interest in both the OTM and ATM products.

Many swing traders are trying to take advantage of reasonably short-term price fluctuations in a sector, and they are likely to choose an OTM opportunity as they expect ITM to go fast, thus enabling them to sell it back. It is because options have time value along with the intrinsic value, and as time grows towards expiration, the time value declines increasingly. This inspires a swing trader to sell back an option that they bought when a reasonable profit represents itself at the first opportunity.

Agree on an Expiration Date

Selecting an expiry date would represent, in part, how long you believe it would take the underlying market to achieve your target price. You'll need to select a shorter-term option if you suppose the transfer would be a longer-term option, especially if you assume it could take more time.

For a swing trader, you simply don't want to have an option that dies so early because it could end up being useless at expiration. On the other side, owing to the comparatively high cost, you do not intend to purchase an option with an expiry date so long in the future.

Often swing traders would pick options or calls for about one month on the near-future market if it is more than a month out since this normally allows them ample room to work out before expiry.

Time Your Entry

The timing of trading entries is usually completed using technical evaluation. Since swing traders deal both with patterns and with adjustments to such patterns, they first must recognize, if any, the dominant pattern in the commodity they are looking at.

Swing traders would go for a remedial pullback while trading with the trend to create a position in trend direction. If the pullback appears to be losing steam, as shown by an RSI level in over-bought or over-sold range, preferably indicating price deviation, they will believe the time to enter the market is ripe.

Carry Out Your Trade

When the time has come for the trade, it's time to proceed according to the trading schedule. For example, if the global trend is above average, you could buy an OTM call option or an OTM put option if the marketplace is downward.

It's always crucial to note that the way you deal is just as critical as the point at which you sell, so make sure you select the best broker as your business companion. Transaction costs can certainly add up over a period, including handling spreads and fees if you regularly trade as a swing dealer.

Manage the Position

You run the risk of failure after you have conducted trade and have a choice, but because you bought an option, the liability would be restricted to the price you paid for it. You may always need to track the underlying demand to better handle the option trade. If you buy an OTM share, you will decide to sell it until the underlying market hits the price of the strike, and it is ATM. If the time value rises, that would also rise in the option of selecting an extra prime.

The decay of time would be struggling with potential gains occurring for each day an option approaches its expiry date. This suggests that at the earliest moment possible, you'll want to sell back the option position to prevent making a deal centered on a perception that directionally seemed risk value due to premature deterioration over time. If the market still seems like your trade would finally pan out, but the short-term change you planned to capitalize on and disastrous to materialize will allow it more time period to come to fruition.

It may be achieved by conducting a calendar roll-out swap that includes selling back your own near-term option and purchasing a longer-term option at a similar strike price. This avoids you from having losses as their expiration approaches because of the greatly increasing time decline on near-money options.

Married Put

An investor purchases an asset in a married put strategy and, at the same time, purchases put options on an equal amount of securities. The buyer of the put option is entitled to sell the stock at the strike price, and the value of each contract is 100 shares.

When keeping a stock, an investor can opt to use this strategy as a way to minimize their downside risk. For instance, suppose an investor buys 100 stock shares and simultaneously buys one put option. In the case of a significant shift in the market price, this approach could be beneficial to this investor since they are shielded from the downside. Around the same moment, if the asset rises in value, the investor will be able to participate in any possibility of upside. The main drawback to this approach is that the investor sacrifices the balance of the premium charged on the put option if the stock does not decrease in value.

Long Butterfly

Butterfly spread options are made up of 2 vertical spreads with a similar strike price. In other terms, an opening position where options (either calls or puts) are acquired (or sold) at 3 separate strike rates includes butterfly options. The method in which these options are produced renders the butterfly a position of both limited losses and limited benefits.

It is possible to build the Long Butterfly spread option using either all call options or all put options. A Long Butterfly formed using call options would work like one generated using put options due to put-call parity. In other terms, it doesn't really matter if you make your Long Butterfly using calls or puts.

Short Iron Condor Strategy

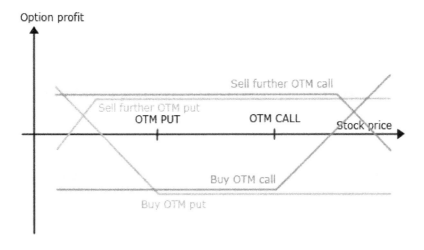

An advanced options trading technique that utilizes a mixture of two vertical spreads is the Iron Condor strategy. At strike prices that are greater than the current price of the underlying stock, a call spread is opened, and a put spread is opened at strike prices, which are lower than the current price.

For volatile stocks, the Short Iron Condor technique is used. It is created by opening up a bullish out-of-the-money (OTM) call spread, and a bearish out-of-the-money (OTM) put spread. You purchase an OTM call, and you sell an extra OTM call. Then you purchase an OTM put then sell an OTM put, which is an extra OTM. This causes a scenario of debit spread, whereby when you open the position, you need to compensate for the difference in premiums.

Long Iron Butterfly Options

The technique of the Iron Butterfly options is an advanced options strategy that uses 2 vertical spreads (1 call spread and 1 put spread) to build a position that is beneficial when you anticipate low volatility or when you require great volatility but are unaware of the direction. The Iron Butterfly is close to the strategies of the Butterfly and Iron Condor, as the name suggests. It has the same profile for-profit and risk as to the Butterfly but uses a mix of option spreads similar to the Iron Condor.

The most widely used variant of the Iron Butterfly is the Long Iron Butterfly option. They are ideal for stocks that would not change significantly (low volatility).

4.2 Avoid common beginner mistakes

You are not forced to buy or to sell while trading options. You actually have the right to trade two kinds of stock options instead: puts and calls. Participants in new options are enthusiastic about the advantage's participants earn and make errors. To avoid errors, you must read about the mistakes made by the option traders.

Starting too Big

Starting too big is the first error most novice options traders make. Start dealing with smaller positions in the business. To start your options trading experience on the right foot, sell a limited number of shares at a time.

Using only one Strategy

Options traders usually start off by trading long and short. Although you could achieve success using this technique, it should not be the only approach you use. Options trading gives you too many innovative options for trading strategy. As a novice, connect with what works for you while studying new techniques simultaneously. Then, this common error that new options traders make can be avoided.

Illogical Expiration Date

Novice traders of options often struggle to realize the expiration's power. Although you have various choices for your expiry date, not all of them are produced equally. You ought to get an attitude first in order to pick the right expiration date for you. Question yourself how long you expect the trade is going to take. Evaluate liquidity. Do not make a premature call about your expiration date to prosper as a novice options trader.

Thinking cheaper is beneficial

By purchasing out-of-the-money, several start-up options traders lose out. Through purchasing out-of-the-money, you hold the premium on an option cheap. When they are told not to go too big, several new buyers opt for this approach. When engaged in options trading, strive to make good choices, not simply cheap choices.

Increasing the number of trades to make up for Losses

Finally, to recoup early losses as an options investor, stay away from doubling up. Once investors like you start trading options, they find it challenging to control losses and leap into trying to catch up. They do that by doubling up in an effort to reduce their cost structure per deal. While this may happen when doubling up, it typically does not. New option traders, instead, end up exacerbating their risk. Close failed trades instead of attempting to solve problems that have already damaged you and your money. When you understand when to close trades, you move a step closer to transitioning from a novice to a good option investor.

Drawdown

During a particular period, a drawdown is a peak-to-trough fall. The percentage between the high and the following low is generally quoted as a drawdown. When a trading account has $10,000 in it, then before going up over $10,000, the assets decrease to $9,000, so the trading account has seen a 10 percent drawdown.

Drawdowns are relevant for calculating the historical risk of various assets, evaluating the performance of investments or tracking the success of personal trading.

As long as the price stays below the top, a drawdown remains in place. In the above case, once the account goes up above $10,000, we don't realize the drawdown is just 10 percent. The drawdown is registered until the account goes up over $10,000.

This way of tracking drawdowns is beneficial since once a new high emerges, a low can't be calculated. As long as the price or value stays below the old rate, a smaller trough might arise that would raise the amount of drawdown.

Draw-downs help assess the financial risk of an investment. The Sterling ratios provide drawdowns to equate the potential benefit of security to its risk.

Although we try our utmost to handle transactions to avoid losers, losses are inevitable. Our aim, as traders, is to reduce the extent and severity of these losses.

Because losses influence the valuation of your investments, which in turn affects your future purchase power, therefore, keeping losses in check is crucial.

Keeping small positions, generating more activities to make the possibilities play out, and uncorrelated trading products are some of the keys to reducing drawdowns.

Time to Recover a Drawdown

While the scale of drawdowns is a risk determination factor, the period it takes to recover a drawdown is also a factor. Not all assets behave equally. Some recuperate better than most. To recover the loss created by a 10 percent drawdown in one hedge fund or trader's account could take years. On the other side, in a short period of time, another hedge fund or investor could very rapidly regain losses, driving the account to peak value. Therefore, drawdowns can often be viewed in light of how long the transaction or fund has usually taken to recover the loss.

Example of a Drawdown

Suppose a trader agrees to purchase $100 of Apple stock. The price increases to $110 (peak) but then decline to $80 (trough) rapidly and then climbs again to $110.

The stock high was $110, and the low was $80. $30 / $110 = 27.3% is the drawdown.

This means that a drawdown is not inherently equivalent to a loss. The stock drawdown was 27.3%, but while the stock was at $80, the trader will display an unrealized loss of 20 percent. This is since, in terms of their buying price ($100 in this case), most traders perceive losses and not the peak price the investment multiplied after entry.

The price then rallies to $120 (peak), continuing with the scenario, and then drops down to $105 before rallying to $125.

The latest peak is currently $120, and $105 for the newest low. This is a drawdown of $15, or $15 / $120 = 12.5%.

How to deal with Drawdowns

Drawdown in trading is an essential part of the method of trading and is of serious importance to traders, particularly beginners. The reality that 100 percent of profit dealing does not occur. Losses follow all, including the most seasoned, with profits. In addition, drawdowns are deemed a very natural part of each trader's trades. This trend is acknowledged by some individuals, and others are indignant towards this. As a consequence, traders, under the control of feelings, lose major ones. Probably, that's why the issue of drawdowns and how a trader can act is worth discussing.

Reasons for drawdowns in trading

The psychology of trading is the most popular explanation for drawdowns in trading. It is also the mental condition that allows drawdowns to emerge, and perhaps, how well a trader is able to communicate with emotions. Gambling, greed, the ability to boost prices and win back losses can affect the outcome. First of all, as those feelings emerge, a trader must know how to control himself and fight. Otherwise, he would lead to a drawdown himself.

The absence of a functional trade mechanism or successful guidelines for entry is another explanation for a drawdown.

This is the second primary explanation for drawdowns of the trader. Intuitive trading takes place, of course, but only if it's founded on several years of trial, error and success experiences. This is not adopted by all, especially inexperienced traders, as experience demonstrates. Beginners are great at taking up a strategy for trading, learning to work with it and adapting it to trading steadily. They need to handle the discipline problem extremely well. Otherwise, drawdowns would be difficult to prevent.

One of the most substantial factors for the appearance of drawdowns is market developments. Usually, the nature of the economy is volatile and unforeseeable. No one should underestimate the market's uncertainty. And if the findings have been optimistic for a long period of time, drawdowns cannot be excluded. They arise as a consequence of price shifts and, as a consequence, the inefficiency of the trading approach. All of this suggests that considering the very market shifts that lead to the drawdowns, the investor has to modify the preferred approach. This is, after all, an entirely normal circumstance. If the market has evolved, then the trading strategy must adapt.

The natural occurrence of drawdowns can be avoided by risk control since this is attributed to the lack of self-discipline, anger management and the development of a determination to recover losses. It is still necessary to deal with your feelings in time and note that without some drawdowns, there is no trading.

Recommendations for drawdowns in trading

Given below are the methods and ways to manage and control drawdowns in trading.

You must remember one important thing that due to the distinctive traits of each individual, each person will have to look for ways to adapt to these recommendations.

Exits

When it comes to drawdowns, we concentrate on our emotionality and responses. A perfect way is to take a time-out and rest your minds from trading. Taking a break is going to really ideally place things in order. Understand, you're not going to lose much in a couple of hours, which is time to calm off. After all, a number of wonderful prospects are always waiting for you; just losing one or two carry no meanings and shall have no impact on your performance. It's better to live with the heat of passion than to risk all the capital.

Self-discipline

Next, we're talking about self-discipline that helps build a trader's diary. This is popular and the easiest and efficient approach. Start registering new deals and outcomes after relaxing and dealing with emotions. You should read up on your errors. You should not be lazy here, knowing that the game is worth the flame and any transaction carefully documented would in the future show the correct direction. This is a waste of time; many people say, because they don't need a diary at all. It is not like that at all, because even trading masters have been maintaining their diaries for years. When the trader falls further and further into a drawdown, it is extremely necessary to maintain a journal.

Manage Stress

The issue of the trader's psychology determines a process, the physical load, which is not always normal, but successful. This is an outstanding strategy for minimizing steam in reaction to each oversight or failure, attempt physical workouts. To expel the unwanted feelings and ideas, others actually have a couple of squats or push-ups. Thus, from the chaotic state, the trader lets himself out. Also, those who do not have the chance to participate in physical exercises for different reasons might try respiratory equipment. Starting trading with a cold head is still the main thing.

Example of dealing with drawdown

There are a variety of ways to help reduce some of the risks to the portfolio of an active trader, and when faced with drawdowns, the top strategies are listed below.

If the investment is in long stock, the first strategy may be carried out. Through selling an out-of-the-money call, the benefit opportunity has been limited, which certainly might put certain investors off. Costs per equity have, however, been decreased.

You have simply reduced the price per share down to $18 a share by purchasing 100 XYZ securities for $20 a share and offering a call on those securities for $2, minimizing the risk in the transaction and converting a buy-and-hope plan into trading with high chance options.

At best, 45-60 days before expiration, you should look at a 30-delta call. That would offer a large sum of credit and also have a 70 % chance of not breaching the call, enabling the investor to roll out the request as time passes and receive even further cash, thereby lowering the trade's cost base.

Furthermore, if you sell a spread of out-of-the-money, and the share price moves in the opposite direction and is in the money now, you might sell the opposing spread.

So this will simply sell a call spread against it if the fund has a short put spread. It generates an iron condor transaction by doing this, but it still helps the trader to bring in an extra trading credit. When you sold a two-dollar wide put spread for fifty cents, then the risk for the initial contract was $150.

You brought in $30 in credit and decreased the trade risk down to $120 by selling the competing call spread for 30 cents. It won't save a deal that's gone bad, though some of the danger will be mitigated.

If both the short and long legs of the trade are in the money on at least three straight trading days, you will apply this adjustment.

The last strategy is to roll out the spread in time. If it's not turned lucrative by 30 days or so before expiration has come, you can choose for this.

This helps you to usually draw in extra credits by rolling out of time and offers your trade 1-2 additional months to turn successful. In order to be right, the aim here is to take in more cash, reduce risk and improve time.

While trading options enable a trader to generate a huge chance of benefit, there is still a risk something might go wrong. Before initiating the trade, getting a strategy in place is the secret. It would help you transact more easily than just purchasing and wishing for the best, by holding the risk per transaction minimal and getting a documented exit goal and adjustment trigger.

When to exit an options trade

It will also support to be much more successful, but it is not important to quit trades early to be profitable. It is also a smart decision to close option positions, especially when they hit 50 percent or another fraction of the max benefit. This isn't known to most traders, so it sounds like a terrible plan. Many traders agree that closing a position at half of the benefit decreases a strategy's total profitability because you get less cash. While it may appear like this is the case, it really is not. It is because closing trades early at a lower benefit generally boosts efficiency and is a really smart idea.

Guaranteed Winners

It will be a guaranteed gain if you leave a trade early for less than max profit. When the position is still at 50 percent of the full value, if you close it, it is a lucrative transaction. This indicates you've made a profit. It is not an assured benefit if you do not close it early. The position will also switch around to become a losing position. Sometimes, keeping trade and aiming to hit maximum profit is not worth the risk. This implies early closing trades would potentially boost your win rate, so as soon as they hit your benefit objective, you need to close trades and don't let them turn into losses.

More Trades

You would be prepared to enter into fresh trading faster if you close positions early. This suggests that with any transaction, you allocate funds for a shorter amount of time. This also increases the number of trades that you can enter into. Premium trading in high-risk options is mostly about the accuracy and having as many transactions as possible. This is precisely what early closing positions would allow. In an expiration loop, you would be ready to take profits sooner and launch fresh ones quicker, thereby trading more in total.

Assignment Risk

You will most likely be allocated far fewer stocks if you want to leave trades early. The less time an option has before its expiry, the more probable it is to be exercised. In the last week of an expiry period, about 80 percent of options are exercised. This is because, in the last week, only a tiny extrinsic time value exists. Therefore, closing out an option contract and then buying the shares would not be more lucrative.

Early closure of options positions would also avoid the last days/weeks of an expiry period and therefore reduce the chance of being assigned. This, without any doubt, is a really positive thing, especially for smaller account traders, who might have difficulty managing an assignment.

Gamma Risk

The Greek Gamma option calculates Delta's rate of shift for each $1 transfer in the underlying. Gamma often varies all the time, much as the price of your option or the underlying. The closest you come to expiration, Gamma rises. What this suggests is that the value of the option contract becomes even more susceptible to market fluctuations in the underlying as you move near to expiration. In the expiration period, Delta can adjust much faster than it did earlier. This suggests that losing/winning chance can, therefore, be more unpredictable. The value of the option contract can increase/decrease far more than earlier in the expiration cycle for every $1 change in the underlying price. For short positions, Gamma is negative, and for long positions, positive. This suggests that the underlying short positions lose more and more of their worth on any $1 shift. For every move, long positions, on the other side, lose less and less. Gamma risk of directional risk, particularly in the last weeks of an expiration period, is something that an option trader should certainly be aware of.

This means that the closest you come to expiration, the more cash you will risk with a slight step in the underlying and the closest you get to expiration, the larger the Gamma rises. You would risk even more from a few dollar shifts in the underlying price prior to expiration (with a high Gamma) than early in the expiration period. This is also the rationale why selling short-term options is not generally quite pleasant, even though time decay is maximum in the last week before expiration.

A Trading Routine Is Vital To Your Success

Habit is what really defines our progress or failure, inclusive of trading in every initiative. So, how do we build the kind of behaviors that will contribute to successful trading for us?

A routine is a remedy.

What are you thinking about when you contemplate your normal trading routine? Have you ever got one? You know that all experts, whether they recognize it or not, have specific procedures and special routines. These schedules and rituals are followed as clockwork, all from food, workout, sleep, and meditation.

After a successful regular trading pattern has become an entrenched practice, it has basically become part of you, and you practically become an 'auto-pilot.'

The power of daily trading routines

You could not make it without a regular trading schedule.

It's not only about making a trading schedule; it's about what you're doing from the moment you wake up to the moment you sleep. It's just part of your everyday trading routine.

A regular routine has been established by experienced traders. This enables them to maximize their capacity to trade efficiently and effectively. What does it look like here? Well, it will certainly differ from one trader to another, but it will be common for all of the components of a normal trading routine: Get a good night's sleep, ideally 7 to 8 hours.

A good and nourishing breakfast is a must.

Analyze the **daily chart trend** of the markets you want to trade at the start of the week.

Find out the **key horizontal support and resistance levels** at the start of the trading week.

Study and analyze your charts of interest daily in the morning. Look for **price action signals** that match with the daily chart trend and support or resistance levels.

Look at your favorite markets soon after the **New York close**. Try to look and spot for visible and potent price action that could have a significant impact on the trend.

If a trading signal compliments your trading plan criteria, take a position and go to sleep till the next morning. If you are unable to spot any lucrative trade, then move away from the screen and take rest till tomorrow morning.

If a trade has not been closed and it is still open, review it in the morning and only notice what has happened, unless there is an apparent, reasonable justification to do so, do not take any action. You should just observe, recall, set up, and forget much of the time.

The above, though brief and plain, is an instance of a smart trading routine. The main point to remember in the above process is that we don't waste any time reviewing or entering transactions on the market. Instead, we treat the business the same way and approximately every day at the same time, because our minds are prepared to start converting this low-maintenance, easy routine and trading treat into a constructive trading habit.

It is important that you establish your own trading pattern, one that makes sense in your everyday life and schedule. For every trader, the same routine would certainly not work.

The lifestyle of an 'end-of-day' trading routine

Not only will trading boost your trading in an end-of-day way, but it will also enable you to have a happier life and enjoy the 'fruits' of trading.

Like the one mentioned above, the trading pattern that many effective traders follow helps us to spend a lot of time of a day away from the charts. After all, having a normal 9 to 5 monotonous, time-consuming career is not part of the reason most of us get into trading, right? So, if you still want independence, you need to trade in an end-of-the-day way.

The science behind routines

A game-changer for imagination is an everyday activity. It keeps tasks continuously simmering in the subconscious, among other items, and studies demonstrate how strong the unconscious mind is, allowing us to make smarter choices than active thinking.

Making a schedule tends to make sure you perform stuff correctly. Not only does a routine benefit you instinctively since it holds you in-tune and closely connected to the most critical tasks you need to do every day (such as reviewing the charts), thereby getting you great at them (think practice), but it would also give you the strongest opportunities to effectively execute

your trading strategy and follow your market participation rules.

Bottom line

Trading is about autonomy, so don't become a hostage to your charts and the markets. Probably one of the trickiest issues traders have to figure out way too much by trial and error is that they must first understand that the only factor they can manage is themselves in order to attain the sort of trading lifestyle they dream of. Spending more time studying and analyzing your charts does not suggest that you would be a successful trader. A laid-back, comfortable and minimalist sort of routine is the trading routine needed to become a good trader who does not over-trade and get sentimental over-trading.

CHAPTER 5: The Benefits of Technical Analysis in Options Trading

Technical analysis is an art that capitalizes on the study of price charts (minute-based, hourly, daily, weekly, monthly or yearly). The underlying basis of this technique is that all markets trend. Why? This is because the prices during their daily undulation-and-fluctuation-phase hit or attain certain highs and lows. These highs and lows of any stock or commodity are then plotted on a chart. The prices, after being plotted, never surface up in a helter-skelter manner on a graph chart.

These prices, when plotted, take the form of a wave. This wavy form is a classic result of prominent crests (highs) and troughs (lows). Eventually, these highs and lows create identifiable points on the chart. These points can be easily joined by a line which is then studied and analyzed for the identification of future price trend and forecasting of price targets. Besides, this technique helps you to timely identify the buying or selling opportunities and thus offers excellent opening and exit points.

5.1 History of Technical Analysis

We shall briefly review the work and contribution of renowned personalities towards the development and creation of a fabulous technique of Technical Analysis.

Charles Henry Dow

Dow is accredited with the invention of the Dow Jones Industrial Index. Besides, he also has the honor of establishing the renowned "The Wall Street Journal," which has now become a financial benchmark for all financial papers.

Dow would record the highs and lows of Index on a daily, weekly, and monthly basis as he did not have the liberty and facility of recording short-term data on the lines as is being conveniently carried out by modern electronic trading software.

Assumptions of Dow Theory

Charles Dow advocated three primary tenets of his theory for analysis of market price and for making future projections or forecasts.

Market Prices Progress in three trends

The first assumption states prices progress in three forms simultaneously. These forms are described as Primary, Secondary, and Minor trends of the price movement. The prior knowledge of the kind or trend of the market price assists a trader to work out a realistic profit-objective and evade early market exit.

Price discounts all

"Price discounts all" means that the market price at which buyers and sellers concur to enter into a trade is a price that has weathered the brunt of all relevant (positive or negative) information presently available to market participants. This information could vary from new economic fundamental data to new developing events, stories, regional conflicts, central banks' initiatives, and policies, etc. Besides, this final price is also reflective of the current emotional and financial status of the participants. Any new information or contradictory information is efficiently "discounted" by the market participants, and the final price tends to portray the current information level and sentiment status of the participants.

History repeats itself

Technical analysis is described as the study and analysis of past price trends to predict and forecast future price movements and trends. Technical analysis of charts is an art used to detect patterns in price movements. These price patterns are then used to predict future market behavior and price targets.

You must understand and remember that the market is not just several shares of various companies exhibiting different price movements. In reality, a market is a collection of human beings who, based on their knowledge, perception, and financial strength, are responsible for the movement of the price in different directions. It is the demand or supply emanating from the people that make the market depict a specific behavior or trend. This essentially shifts the price!

You will be wrong in your assessment if you think that the sole reason behind a positive movement in the stock price of a company is the significant gains in last year's profits. The price of the stock goes up because profit news is conceived positively by the market participants, and consequently, they jump in with their funds to buy that stock. The human beings demand stoked by specific factors propels upward movement in prices. This is a very critical concept in your knowledge of technical analysis.

Human psychology remains constant and manages to respond to related situations identically. The study and analysis of the past market behavior at turning points are incredibly beneficial and advantageous in the identification of specific price patterns for the development of an understanding of the market's most probable future reaction. Hence, technical analysis assumes that people will persist in doing the same blunders that they did in the past. Human Being relationships are incredibly complicated. The markets, as explained above, reflect people in action, never duplicating their presentation exactly. Still, the recurrence of identical features is necessary to make it easier for market watchers to recognize notable junctions or turning points.

Technical analysis banks on the study of market action, which in turn is contingent upon the study of human psychology. Different chart patterns have established their authenticity as a result of the review of their effectiveness in all types of markets. These patterns continue to appear on charts with a regular frequency depending on the particular trend of the market. These patterns reveal the bullish or bearish psychology of the market participants. The past utility of these price patterns in generating excellent trading profits makes them viable and tenable for future decision making. Hence the key to knowing the future lies in the analysis of the past, or the future is a mere mirror image of the past.

Market Trend and Types

Dow Theory helps in:

Identifying the existence of a trend

Deciphering the direction of the trend

Classifying the phase of the trend

A trend can be identified by merely joining the two points with the help of a line and then extending that line to see if it meets other points to establish its validity.

If the market is registering higher highs and lows, then the upward slanting line is drawn, which reflects the positive or bullish trend in the market. On the contrary, if the market is making lower highs and lows, then a downward slanting line tells about the negative or bearish trend of the market.

Movement of prices from a trough or bottom to crest or a peak is categorized as a rally, while the downside movement from a peak to bottom is defined as a sell-off in the market. The diagram below demonstrates the upward and downward trends with associated rallies and sell-offs, and vice versa.

A market trend is characterized by the presence of three intermittent trends or phases:

Major or Primary Trend or Phase

The core job of a technical analyst is to identify the major direction or long-term trend of the market with the help of different price patterns and tools. This is typically the most critical aspect of technical analysis because it enables the trader to ensure the optimal ride of the wavelength, which translates into the maximization of trade profit. The long term trend usually lasts for one to three years with some variations.

Secondary Trend or Phase

Sell-off or corrections or retracements in the primary trend defines the secondary trend of the market. If the underlying trend is bullish, then any erosion in prices marked by price movement in the opposite direction of the prime trend is classified as a market correction or retracement in the prime trend.

On the contrary, markets in primary bearish or downward trend shall exhibit upward corrective or secondary bullish trends. The secondary trend comparatively has a short time span of three weeks to three months. The technical analyst makes use of the Fibonacci retracement tool to work out the correction or retracement in a given market.

Minor or Consolidative Trend or Phase

The last phase is characterized by the development of minor trends resulting from small corrections within the secondary trend. The direction of prices during the minor trend is always against the direction of the secondary trend. This is typically one of the most tedious phases, and ignorant and hasty traders tend to lose a lot of money in this phase because of choppy price behavior.

However, a technical analyst who is aware of the bigger picture either avoids trading during this phase of the market or keeps his financial commitment minimal. This is because excessive trading in this phase can result in distraction, and you can ultimately be deprived of enjoying the lucrative monetary benefits of major trends.

5.2 Fibonacci Retracement

Fibonacci identified the sequence of numbers that were translated into mathematical relationships and subsequently converted into ratios. These ratios are applied to calculate the approximate length of corrective waves. Fibonacci retracement works by applying the following ratios/percentages to the value arrived at by measuring the distance between a peak or crest and a trough or bottom:

23.6% or 0.236

33% or 0.382

50% or 0.50

61.8% or .618 or 66%

100% (sometimes the markets retrace the total length of the preceding wave)

The identification of retracement levels facilitates the identification of support and resistance levels. This is usually done by drawing horizontal lines at each peak or retracement level. An efficient trader shall use these support and resistance levels to maximize trade profits by astutely defining his entry and exit points.

5.3 Characteristics of technical analysis

The salient characteristics of technical analysis are:

The primary feature of technical analysis requires the usage of price and volume adjustment formulas and trading laws, such as moving averages, RSI, regressions, business cycles, and intraday market trend trends, stock market fluctuations, or chart trend identification.

Unlike fundamental analysis that takes into consideration the company fact market, currency, or commodity, technical analysis measures price, volume, and related market statistics.

Finally, technical analysis is commonly used by traders and financial professionals and is also utilized by aggressive day traders, pit traders, and market makers.

5.4 Types of charts

There are three types of charts that are more commonly used in technical analysis. These are:

Japanese Candlestick Charts

Throughout the 17th century, the Japanese started using scientific analyzes to exchange grains. Although this early iteration of the theoretical review differs from Charles Dow's US iteration introduced about 1900, much of the basic concepts were quite similar:

The "what" (price action) is more important than the "why" (news, earnings, and so on).

All known information is reflected in the price.

Buyers and sellers move markets based on expectations and emotions (fear and greed).

Markets fluctuate.

The actual price may not reflect the underlying value.

Formation of Candlesticks

In order to construct a chart of a candlestick, you must provide a collection of data that includes accessible, large, low and near values for each time frame you want to view. The hollow or loaded candlestick part is called "the core" (also known as "the true core"). The long thin lines above and below the body reflect the high/low scale, which is regarded as "shadows" (also regarded as "wicks" which "tails"). The high is marked by the peak of the upper shadow and the low by the lower shadow's edge. If the stock closes over its starting price, a hollow candlestick will be drawn. The body bottom reflects the price of the opening, and the body top reflects the price of the closure. If the stock ends below the opening price, the top of the body is illustrated with a loaded candlestick reflecting the opening

price and the bottom of the body showing the closing price.

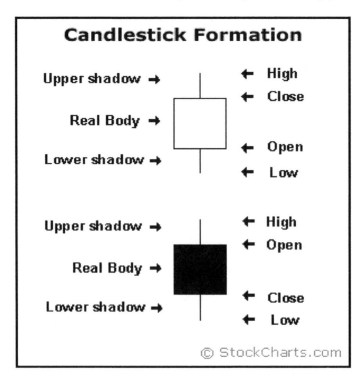

5.5 Hollow candlesticks patterns

Long and Short Bodies

In fact, the longer the body becomes, the more severe the desire to purchase or sell. In comparison, the small candlesticks show no change in prices and reflect consolidation.

Although long white candlesticks are usually bullish, their place within the wider technical picture depends greatly. Long white candlesticks will label a possible tipping point or degree of assistance after sustained decreases. When after a long advance, the buying is too violent, it may contribute to unnecessary bullishness.

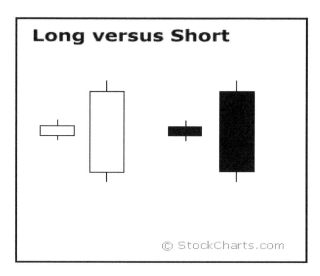

© StockCharts.com

The bigger the black candlestick is, the farther down the open the closure is. This suggests a major drop in rates from the free, yet hostile sellers. A long black candlestick can foreshadow a turning point after a long advance, or mark a future level of resistance. A long black candlestick may indicate panic, or capitulation, after a long decline.

Long and Short Shadows

On candlesticks, the upper and lower shadows will provide useful trading session detail. Upper shadows represent the session low with high and lower shadows. Short shadowed candlesticks suggest that much of the trading activity was contained to the open and close. Long shadowed candlesticks show that prices went well past the open and close.

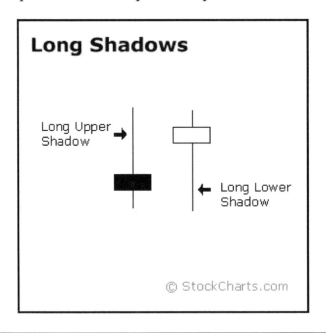

Candlesticks with a long upper shadow and a shorter lower shadow indicate buyers dominated during the session, bidding higher prices, but sellers eventually forced down prices from their highs. This clear comparison of high and low closeness culminated in a long upper shadow. In comparison, candlesticks with long lower shadows and short upper shadows suggest sellers prevailed throughout the session, pushing down costs. Nevertheless, buyers subsequently resurfaced to offer prices higher by the end of the session, along with lower shadow generated by the fast close.

Tall upper shadowed candlesticks, large lower shadow, and tiny actual body are known as spinning tops. One long shadow is a reverse of sorts; spinning tops are indeterminate. The tiny actual body (whether hollow or filled) reveals no change from open to near, and the shadows suggest that during the session, both bears and bulls were involved.

Doji

Doji represents an important type of candlestick, providing information both on their own and as elements of several key forms. When a security's open and close are nearly identical, Doji type, the duration of the upper and lower shadows will differ, with a cross, inverted triangle or plus sign appearing like the resulting candlestick. Together, neutral trends are doji. The previous market behavior and potential evidence form the foundation of every bullish or bearish bias. The term "Doji" applies to the singular as well as the plural form.

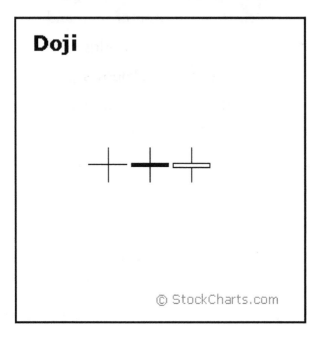

A dog's relevance depends on the previous pattern or the candlesticks before it. A Doji indicates after an advance that the purchasing momentum is starting to diminish. A Doji indicates after a decline that the sales pressure is starting to decrease.

Long-Legged Doji

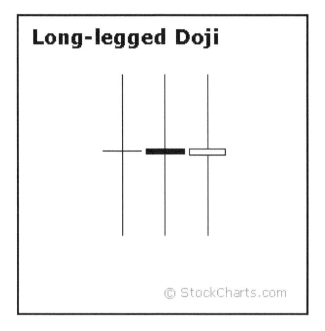

Long-legged Doji has long shadows, upper and lower, which are almost identical in length. This Doji represents a significant amount of business indecision. Long-legged Doji show rates exchanged both above and below the opening stage of the session but were practically closed even with the free. The final product, despite a whole bunch of shouting and crying, shows no improvement from the original available.

Dragonfly Doji and Gravestone Doji

When the open, high, and close are equal, the Dragonfly Doji is formed, and the low creates a long, lower shadow. Owing to the absence of an upper shadow, the resultant candlestick appears like a "T" Dragonfly Doji shows trade was controlled by sellers and pushed prices down throughout the session. By the end of the day, investors resurfaced and moved prices down to the day high and opening stage.

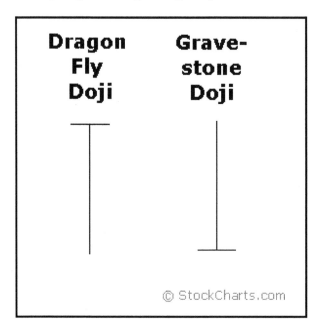

A dragonfly doji's reversal effects rely on prior market behavior and potential confirmation. The long lower shadow is indicative of purchasing demand, but the low shows that there are already plenty of sellers lingering. If the open, short, and close are similar, the Gravestone Doji type and the high produces a long upper shadow. Despite the absence of a lower eye, the resultant candlestick appears like an upside-down "T" Gravestone Doji suggests investors have controlled dealing and pushed higher prices throughout the session. However, sellers resurfaced and pushed prices back to opening and low session levels by the end of the session. As with the dragon fly doji and other candlesticks, Gravestone doji's reversal effects depend on previous market behavior and potential confirmation. Even though the long upper shadow suggests a failed rebound, there is some buying interest at the intraday level. Following a long downtrend, long black candlestick, or at help, attention shifts to proof of purchasing interest and a possible bullish upturn. The emphasis switches to the missed rally and a possible bearish turnaround after a lengthy uptrend, long white candlestick or opposition. Confirmation of Bearish or Bullish is required for both situations.

Hammer and Hanging Man

The Hammer and Hanging Man look exactly the same, but, based on the preceding price action, have different implications. They have actual thin limbs, lengthy lower shadows and limited or non-existent upper shadows (black or white). As for most configurations of single and double candlesticks, the Hammer and Hanging Man need approval before practice.

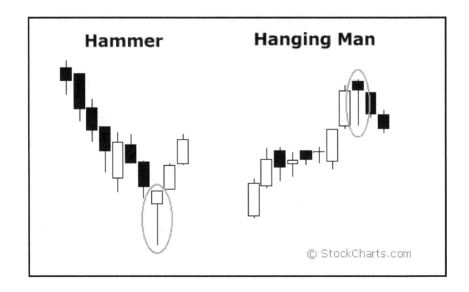

The Hammer is a bullish trend of turnaround, evolving after a fall. Besides a potential reversal of the pattern, hammers may even label bottoms or help rates. Hammers have indicated an optimistic resurgence following a fall. The long lower shadow's low suggests sellers pushed down rates throughout the session. The strong finish, though, indicates buyers have regained their footing to end the session on a strong note. Although this may seem appropriate to operate on, the hammers need more bullish proof. The hammer's low indicates there are still plenty of sales remaining. Further purchasing pressure is required before operating, and ideally on an increasing scale. Such confirmation may come from a white candlestick up the gap or large. Hammers are close to sale climaxes, and high volume may help to improve reversal validity.

The Hanging Man is a bearish pattern of reversal, which can also mark a level of top or resistance. A Hanging Man, forming after an advance, signals selling pressure is beginning to increase. The long lower shadow's low suggests sellers were driving down prices throughout the session. With the bulls regaining their feet and pushing up rates by the end, the emergence of sales pressure lifts the yellow flag. As with the Hammer, bearish affirmation is expected by a Hanging Man before the intervention. This clarification will arrive on a heavy volume like a gap down or long black candlestick.

Inverted Hammer and Shooting Star

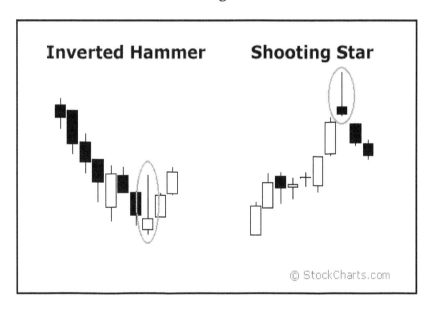

The Inverted Hammer and Shooting Star appear almost the same but, depending on past pricing activity, have distinct consequences. All candlesticks include actual thin bodies (black or white), large upper shadows, and lower shadows, which are tiny or absent. These candlesticks mark potential reversals of the pattern but require proof before practice.

Depiction of Bulls Vs. Bears

A candlestick is a reflection of the fight between Bulls (buyers) and Bears (sellers) over a given time. The comparison can be created between two football teams of this fight, which we may often name the Bulls and the Bears. The candlestick's bottom (intra-session low) reflects a touchdown for the Bears and a touchdown for the Bulls' peak (intra-session high). The higher the rise, the higher the Bulls are to a touchdown. The higher the bottom is, the higher the Bears are to a touchdown.

(Candlesticks showing up and down movement in the S&P 500 index)

Western Bar Charts

One of the fundamental methods of technical analysis is the bar map, where the open, near, strong, and low values of stocks or other financial securities are displayed in bars that are illustrated as a sequence of values over a specified period of time. To differentiate such charts from more conventional bar charts used to represent other forms of data, bar charts are also referred to as OHLC charts (open-high-low-close charts).

Bar charts make it easier for the traders to see patterns. In other terms, each bar is, in reality, just a collection of 4 prices for a certain day, or any other time span, that is linked in a certain way by a bar — hence it is sometimes referred to as a price bar.

A price bar displays the opening price of the financial instrument as a left horizontal line, which is the price at the beginning of the time cycle, and the closing price as a right horizontal line, which is the last price for the duration. Such horizontal lines are classified as tick marks too. The top of the bar reflects the maximum quality, while the bottom of the bar portrays the low price. Unless the pricing bar is a constant price bar for a product, then the opening and closing rates are the sale values at the market opening and at the market closing, respectively. The high price is also the peak demand exchanged during the day, while the low price is the lowest price during the day.

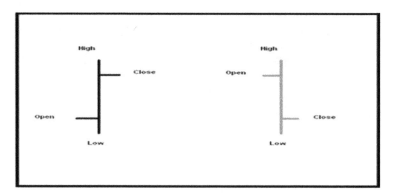

Bar Chart Patterns

Examination of the bar charts becomes more valuable as the bars are presented over a span of time, enabling the discernment of trends that can predict potential values with different degrees of effectiveness. The easiest analogy is between 2 consecutive bars. An up-day is when the closure is higher than the prior day. When the near is smaller, a down-day is. The closing price is usually regarded to be the most critical amount, as traders responded for the day to the news. But often the close is down, not because of poor reports, but because often traders sell overnight due to bad reports on close to prevent any market declines.

Higher closures usually suggest a bullish market feeling while lower closings show a bearish market feeling. An uptrend is a sequence of changes in which the peaks are mostly higher than the day before, and the lows are higher too. The uptrend is supported by both the lows higher and the closes higher (up-day). A downtrend is a reverse cycle, where peaks, drops, and closings on consecutive down-days are typically smaller.

Line Charts

The most common and easiest form of stock charts used in technical analysis is a line map. The line chart is often called a close-only map as it charts the underlying security's closing price, with a line connecting the dots created by the close point. On a line map, the market data for the underlying protection is plotted along the horizontal axis on a graph with the period plotted from left to right, or the x-axis and demand values plotted from the bottom up to the vertical axis, or the y-axis.

Inline charts, the price data used is typically the near price of the underlying security. The line chart's uncluttered simplicity is its greatest asset as it offers a simple, clearly identifiable, graphic representation of the price shift. This makes it an ideal tool for identifying the prevailing levels of support and resistance, trend lines, and certain patterns in the chart.

The line chart does not, however, indicate the highs and lows, and thus do not indicate the session price range. Despite this, line charts were Charles Dow's favorite charting technique, which was only interested in the level at which the price was closed. This, Dow thought, is the session or trading period's most valuable price details, as it calculated the unrealized benefit or loss of that time.

Numerous traders who believe that the closing price is the most relevant data and are not concerned with the uncertainty generated by market fluctuations and small price changes, or the volatility that characterizes the start of the trading day, tend to prefer line charts or close-only charts.

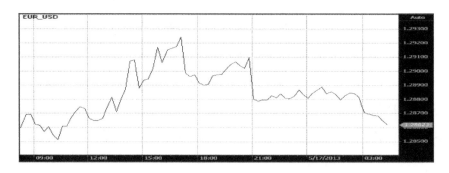

The above is a chart of the EUR/USD with a 15-minute **time frame**.

5.6 Application of Technical analysis for trading Options and its Benefits

In short term trading, technical indicators are also used to enable the investor to recognize the trend and its trajectory.

Since options are prone to time decay, the retention period takes on value. A stock trader is allowed to retain a position forever, while an options trader is constrained by the fixed time specified by the expiry date of the options. Due to time constraints, momentum indicators are common among options traders, which appear to identify levels of overbought and oversold.

Relative Strength Index – RSI

For options on specific securities, RSI fits well. The strongest candidates for short-term trading dependent on RSI are the options for extremely liquid, high-beta stocks.

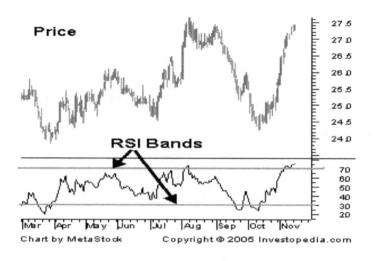

Bollinger Bands

The value of volatility is known to all options traders, and Bollinger bands are a common way to calculate volatility. When volatility rises, the bands extend and contract when volatility declines. The more the price travels to the upper band, the more the security can be overbought, and the more the price rises to the lower band, the more it may be oversold.

A shift of prices beyond the bands will indicate that the security is ripe for a turnaround, and traders of options should position themselves appropriately.

Intraday Momentum Index – IMI

For high-frequency option traders seeking to gamble on intraday movements, the Intraday Momentum Index is a strong technical indicator. It incorporates the principles of intraday candlesticks and RSI, thereby offering an acceptable range for intraday trading (similar to RSI) by suggesting degrees of overbought and oversold. Utilizing IMI, an options trader could be able to spot possible opportunities at an intraday correction to execute a bullish trade in an up-trending market or to execute a bearish trade at an intraday price bump in a down-trending market.

Money Flow Index – MFI

A momentum indicator that incorporates price and volume data is the Money Flow Index. It is often referred to as RSI volume-weighted. The MFI metric calculates the cash inflow and outflows into an asset over a specified period of time.

MFI is best adapted for stock-based options trading (as opposed to index-based) and longer-duration trades due to reliance on volume data. This may be a leading sign of a trend transition as the MFI moves in the same direction as the stock price.

Put-Call Ratio (PCR) Indicator

Using put options against call options, the put-call ratio calculates trading volume. The shifts in its value, regardless of the actual put-call ratio's value, signify a shift in general market sentiment.

The ratio is above 1 when there are more puts than calls, suggesting bearishness. The ratio is less than 1, suggesting bullishness, while call volume is greater than put volume. The put-call ratio, however, is often regarded by traders as a contrary measure.

Open Interest – OI

Open interest shows possibilities for open or unsettled contracts. OI does not generally imply a particular uptrend or downtrend, but it does include indicators of a given trend's intensity. Rising open interest implies fresh capital inflow and, thus, the longevity of the current trend, while a slowing pattern implies a declining OI.

5.7 Mindset and Trading Psychology

Trading of securities is about profit, stop-loss and benefit. On the opposite, trading in options is about a time frame and potential opportunities. Your emphasis is at the initial price at which you execute your order and your profit and loss. You concentrate on static points and an unknown point in time for the opportunity or loss to be created by the trade.

From the outset, options trades are built to recognize how the outcome looks and how long you have to wait to make that outcome happen. Many trade options provide a window of opportunity during which they can earn money in a trade and gain a return in several situations. You make a directional decision in stock markets. Only one scenario creates a return.

The trading of options depends on keeping and changing before the end. Under a "price tent," keep and adjust over a given defined time frame. The emphasis is on the end target, and changes are anticipated and scheduled. In a price range, you work the trade and, if appropriate, change the window before the trade period has elapsed.

Trading psychology explained

One of the most important factors of being a successful trader is having the right mindset. Trading psychology relates to the mentality of an investor during his time in the markets. It will assess the degree to which they are effective in securing a profit, or it may offer an indication of why heavy losses have been suffered by a trader.

The primary goal of studying about trading psychology is to become conscious of the different dangers identified with a significant negative trait and to establish more optimistic qualities. Traders well-versed in the dynamics of investing would normally not operate on prejudice or sentiment. Therefore, they are more likely to produce a return throughout their tenure on the exchanges or to mitigate their losses.

Improve your trading psychology

By being conscious of your own feelings, perceptions and personality characteristics, enhancing your trading psychology will most effectively be accomplished. When these have been identified, you should put in place a trading strategy that takes these variables into consideration in the hope of minimizing any effects they may have on your decision-making.

For example, rather than incurring a minor loss on your trading portfolio, you might let losses run with the expectation that the market would rebound. This might result in higher losses.

You may use stops to offset this to decrease your risks and to determine when to close a certain transaction before you open the trade. By doing so, when you have made a deliberate effort not to rely on them, but rather, you have taken action to counteract them, you have become mindful of your own prejudices and thoughts.

Biases are a personal inclination in favor of one item over another. This is because trading preference means that you will be more likely to trade an asset on which you have had prior performance or to avoid an asset on which a historical loss has occurred. It is necessary for traders to be mindful of their conscious prejudices.

Identify your personality traits

Recognizing your personality traits from the outset is one of the secrets to delivering successful trading psychology. If you have impulsive behavior or if you are inclined to behaving out of indignation or irritation, you would need to be realistic with yourself.

Develop and follow a trading plan

To ensure that you accomplish your targets, having a trading strategy is paramount. A trading plan serves as the template for your trading, and your time obligations, trading funds available, your risk-reward ratio, and a trading strategy you are secure with should be illustrated.

Be adaptive

While having a trading strategy is critical, note that no two days are the same on the markets. If there is more uncertainty on one day and the markets change, especially unpredictably, you can plan to place your trading operation on pause before you are confident that you know what is happening.

Bottom line

Trading psychology is more about your attitude, and it will inform an indication of your gains or losses. Before initiating a trade, it is necessary for you to be mindful of your own

shortcomings and prejudices, but it is also vital that you recognize your own strengths.

Conclusion

Trading in options is generally about getting an advantage against other traders, and you are instantly ahead by narrowly restricting your trades to companies and sectors that you recognize and have studied.

The majority of people claim it is dangerous to trade options and purchase calls/puts. Nevertheless, it is a mistaken idea that traders can easily mint money from options trading or go bankrupt. Uninformed individuals who claim this tend to pursue the assumption that when they expire out of the money, such that, below the calls' strike price and above the strike price of puts, 80% of options expire without profit. This is dead wrong; as prior to expiration, many options are executed.

This would rely a great deal on what your risk level is, how aged you are, what platform you use, and so on. Just 2-5 percent of your portfolio should be devoted to a single trade. There are examples of traders who bet on trades a couple hundred thousand dollars. It is strongly recommended to avoid making such a mistake. Even if you are completely fine about it, you must not ruin your investments.

Each option has a date of expiry — a date that is either worth value or meaningless to that option. An option has no worth when its call option's strike price is greater than the price of the underlying, and when the strike price is below the price of the underlying contract, it is worth something (in the money). At any moment, you can execute the options, but if they are in the money, they will be immediately exercised at their expiry.

Then arises the issue of when the options can be exercised. If you deal with huge capital, the chances are that you're just going to be trading premiums. If you have the funds to really exercise (buy 100 stock shares at the strike price), then if you exercise rather than indulge in option's trading, or are out of the money, and are optimistic on the market, you can gain more money, so go ahead and exercise anytime you like.

You should have a specified timetable when entering an options activity. If you have no idea when you intend to sell or what you intend to do if the underlying falls to x value, almost every time, definitely, you would utterly collapse and lose cash. Take the revenue you earn, take the gain if you earn 100 percent+ on a transaction.

Although there are loads of indicators correlated with options that traders stand by, you can rely on four key indicators.

Delta can assess the option's vulnerability to market fluctuations of the underlying stock. Usually, this would be defined as a number between 1 and -1, where 0 to 1 is for calls, and -1 to 0 is for puts. The scale demonstrates how high the price of the option will increase if the price of the underlying commodity is moved to $1.

Gamma is the rate of a shift in the variance of an option per 1-point shift in the value of the underlying stock. In order to retain a hedge over a larger price spectrum, a delta hedge approach aims to minimize gamma.

Mathematically, gamma is the first delta derivative that is used in an effort to calculate the market change of an option compared to the sum of money it is in or out of. In the same respect, with respect to the underlying interest, gamma is the second derivative of an option's price. Gamma is minimal when the option being determined is deep in or out of the money. When the option is close or at the money, gamma is at its best. For minor adjustments in the price of the underlying stock, Gamma measurements are the most reliable. The long-position options include a positive gamma, whereas a negative gamma is valid for all short options.

Theta is a calculation of an option's time decay, the dollar sum an option would eliminate due to the passing of time every day. Theta grows when an option hits the end date for in the money options. Theta falls when an option reaches expiration for in the money and out of the money options.

Theta is one of the essential terms to be grasped by a beginning options investor since it describes the influence of time on the price of the bought or sold options. Buying longer-term contracts are preferable if you choose to buy an option. You'll like to short the shorter-term options if you want a plan that benefits from time decay because the reduction of value attributable to time occurs fast.

Before initiating an options trade, the first task is to understand what options are and how they will work with the overall trading plan. You may create trading ideas that fit with a particular approach for options with an understanding of how options operate. After a possible trade-in option has been identified, you can build a detailed strategy that includes developing an entry and exit plan. If you can discipline yourself to monitor and manage a trade after its initiation, you can definitely maximize your likelihood of a lucrative outcome.

PART 2

Forex Trading

The Ultimate Guide to Become a Successful Trader. Learn Fundamental and Technical Analysis and Discover the Broker's Role. Build the Right Mindset to Make Money and Create Passive Income.

Andrew Bennett

Introduction

The forex market will give traders from all areas of life excellent opportunities. Reasonable profits on the investment can be made, and several individuals effectively manage to transform their trading practices into full-time employment or high second incomes.

Forex trade is nothing more than trading various foreign currency forms through direct entry, if you were curious. In the past, however, foreign exchange dealing was largely confined to big banks and institutional traders. Recent technical developments have made it so that small traders can now reap the benefits of the many advantages of forex trading easily by trading on the numerous online trading platforms.

The ability to gain from the comparatively minor volatility and shifts in currency prices ensures that everyone can go on trading with the large variety of traditional and online tools/applications currently available; it is relatively easy to set up and start trading.

The world's currencies are at a free exchange rate and are often exchanged in Euro/Dollar, Dollar/Yen pairs. Trading of the main currencies requires approximately 85 percent of all regular trades.

For investing purposes, four major currency pairs are typically used. They are the U.S. dollar against the euro, the U.S. dollar against the Japanese yen, the U.S. dollar against the British pound, and the U.S. dollar against the Swiss franc. We will show you how the trading market feels right now: EUR/USD, USD/JPY, GBP/USD, and USD/CHF. As a reminder, you should realize that no currency dividends are charged.

If you agree that one currency would rise against some other currency, you should swap the second currency for the first currency and continue in it. If all goes as you expect, you will finally be willing to make the reverse offer so that you will trade this first currency for the other currency and then gain money from it.

Dealers at big banks or FOREX trading firms carry out trades in the FOREX industry. FOREX is an essential aspect of the global economy, but traders in Europe exchange currency with their Japanese equivalents while you sleep in the warmth of your home.

It is also rational for you to assume that the FOREX business operates 24 hours a day and that traders work 24/7 in three separate shifts at major institutions. For overnight implementation, clients can position take-profit and avoid loss orders with brokers.

In the FOREX sector, exchange fluctuations are very consistent and without the differences, you find on the equity market almost every morning. There is just near $1.2 trillion in regular trading on the FOREX.

The sector, meaning a fresh trader can buy and leave positions without any difficulties.

The irony is that the FOREX trade never ends, and you might always get your hands on two-sided currency quotations back on September 11, 2001. The world's biggest and oldest stock market is the money market. That is sometimes referred to as the foreign exchange sector, short for F.X. market. It is the world's largest and most liquid economy and is mainly exchanged in the inter-bank currency market 24 hours a day.

If you equate them, you can find that just one percent is as high as the currency futures sector. Trading currencies are not clustered on an exchange, unlike futures and capital markets. Trading travels from big U.S. financial hubs to Australia and New Zealand, the Far East, Europe, and then the U.S.

In the past, because of the broad minimum volume volumes and stringent financial criteria, the forex inter-bank sector was not open to small speculators.

The principal traders were corporations, big currency dealers, and often even very large speculators. They were only willing to take advantage of the currency market's extraordinary strength and the deep trending value of many of the world's primary currency exchange rates.

Today, foreign exchange market brokers can split down larger inter-bank units and give the ability to purchase or sell any amount of these smaller units to small traders like you and me. These brokers offer traders of any sort, whether individual speculators or smaller businesses, the right to exchange at the same prices and price movements as the major players who once ruled the sector.

The foreign exchange industry has come a long way, as you can see. When you are new to the game, being good at it can be intimidating and challenging. Let this be your detailed guide to the forex market being successful.

The purpose of this book, intended for Forex beginners, is to provide a detailed understanding of how the Forex market operates, how successful returns can be produced, and to introduce many of the technical terms and tools that are necessary for regular trading operations.

CHAPTER 1: Forex Trading Basics

There are several words that traders use that may often make it feel like the business has a 'language' of its own, and when beginning out, this may be frustrating. For any dealer, an appreciation of this expert language is a critical baseline.

Offers, Bids, and Spreads:

There will still be two values for each currency pair at every point while interacting with currency trading in the Spot Forex sector. These two values are regarded as the bid and deal price, and the discrepancy is defined as the gap between both. The distinction between these two principles is crucial to consider since they are critical in all trading strategies.

Big Lesson: The bid price will be the quoted amount at which you will offer currency, and when you choose to buy currency, the offer/ask is the amount you will be quoted. The bid price would often be smaller than the bid/ask price, and it is this spread among the two rates that helps trades to favor brokers and market makers.

Margins:

It is not essential to provide an account currently financed with $100,000 to control a ton of currency with an equal amount.

Instead, a trader needs you to have an amount or account investment after the collateral application, to which this leverage can be added as you sell.

What is regarded as the Account Margin is this amount or deposit. This deposit's worth would depend on the form of account kept by your broker's precise criteria and your particular choice. In the event of a deal utilizing 100:1 leverage, the necessary account margin will be a minimum of one percent. So if you were to perform an order at 100:1 for a regular lot ($100,000), then you will have to have a total of $1,000 as a margin to continue. Brokers would also demand that the portfolio be adequately financed beyond the account margin to cover future losses from any excess sum available.

Leverage:

The double-edged weapon in Forex dealing is leverage. Although on the one side, it offers retail traders the ability to make significant gains from the currency markets, it may also contribute to circumstances uncontrolled losses. It Can greatly outweigh initial investments by leveraging only reasonably minor currency price movements.

Knowing the ramifications of leverage, how it functions, and how it can be employed successfully can prove to be immensely advantageous over time. Understanding it involves learning to maximize leverage in a way that offers the highest possible possibility of profit-making and decreases the probability and loss-accumulating chances.

By design, leveraging is a tool that enables a trader to lend and manage much more significant quantities of collateral, using just a comparatively limited sum of private investment. Traders may enter into trades with this specific fund, compounded to provide ownership to a much greater currency stake when leveraged.

This suggests that from comparatively minor currency market fluctuations, gains may be produced. The crucial thing to note is that leveraging operates in all ways because leverage can boost all revenues in the same way; any losses can also be quickly compounded.

In reality, each time you perform a trade order, leverage can be utilized.

You would be allowed to choose the degree of leverage you would like to add to the deal while making an order and this will decide the sum of currency you eventually manage. The margin is defined as the sum of money that you individually have to bring into the deal. This balance would have to be present inside your account until the transaction on your side is conducted by a trader.

An illustration of leverage in reality:

Assume that you have $1,000 that you choose to spend in a specific currency pair, and you plan to enter into a long-term purchase transaction. When you position your order, based on the type of account you have, the broker can offer you a range of leveraging choices. We will use a 100:1 degree of leverage for this case. This means that your $1,000 expenditure is compounded by 100, granting you currency power of $100,000. The currency level is then added to the exchange, and you technically reach the business keeping the sum to buy. Suppose you have calculated as you close the exchange accurately, and the currency price has risen over time. The price rise is added to the $100,000 rather than the $1,000 margin number, thus considerably raising the benefit. Alternatively, if the demand is underestimated and the stock closes lower throughout the exchange, any gains are equally influenced by the same leverage. This will mean you are sacrificing money in the margin and all accrued losses over and beyond the margin stage. Should the market turn against you, stop orders will be used to decrease the losses. In later pages, this sort of order would be addressed in more depth.

Important Lesson: The following alert would be a comment that you will frequently hear during your stock trading:

This is a leveraged object that will contribute to damages that outweigh the original deposit. Forex trading may not be appropriate for everyone, so please make sure you fully comprehend the risks associated.'

In your peril, ignore this!

The probability of financial losses can be minimized by keeping this statement at the forefront of your mind and adding caution any time you deal.

Pips:

In Forex, the word pip represents the value shift between currency pairs as they step up or down. For instance, if the GBP/USD value changes from 1.5125 to 1.5126, then one pip reflects the gradual movement.

A currency's calculated value would typically be expressed in four decimal positions, and this fourth decimal position digit movement is equivalent to one pip. This is the 1/100 equivalent of one percent or one basis point for most currency pairs. Some brokers record currency prices at five decimal points and each change would reflect a tenth of a pip while this is the case. It is sometimes regarded as a pipette at times.

Each currency has its value, and therefore there is a fixed procedure to follow to determine the equal value of a pip: .0001 divided by the exchange rate = Pip value. There are several anomalies in the valuation of pips, particularly in currency pairs that involve the Japanese Yen, since they are sometimes quoted only in two decimal places.

Brokers can measure the pip amount on your behalf, so knowing the underlying mechanism is helpful since it is essentially this aggregation of pips that will impact the benefit or loss selling estimate.

The Lots:

The Spot Forex market is exchanged in batches when it comes to real trading orders. There are tons of several sizes, including Regular, Small, Medium, and Nano, each of which comprises various currency unit numbers.

Many functions are utilizing the ideas of leverage that we have already addressed. They structure the unique sums for each exchange that can be added. Every lot is built from currency units that essentially convert into real-term quantities, so a typical lot consisting of 100,000 units would be equal to $100,000 in regulating monetary value, etc.

Types of Order:

It is essential to include guidance as to the amount and manner by which exchange should be performed to carry out either the purchasing or the selling of the currency. The mixture of these orders is referred to as a command. There are four key forms of order, and it is crucial to be mindful of each one's essence and consequences.

Balance of the Business:

The market order, also often referred to as a free order, is an offer to purchase or sell at the best selling price possible. This suggests that, based on whether the exchange is for a buy or a selling, a trade would be conducted automatically at either the latest offer price or bid price. Therefore if the offer price for GBP/USD is 1.5673 and the offer price is 1.5675, you can purchase at 1.5675 and sell at 1.5673 for a market order.

Limit-Order Entry

The limit-entry order is an instruction to purchase below the current market price at a certain level or an instruction to offer above the current market price at a certain level. Limits may be defined as either a buy limit order or a sale limit order, based on the individual order's path.

You should use this sort of order to guarantee that you don't lose the chance to make a trade. They are also extremely beneficial in enforcing a particular trading plan since they ensure that entry and benefit goals can be established and implemented appropriately.

In general, restricted orders cost more to use than market orders, but the trader's advantages always exceed the added cost.

Stop Order

When the price exceeds a predetermined amount, the stop order is a command for purchasing or sale. This ensures that it may be used to reduce future losses or locking-in lucrative profits to set entry and exit goals. The stop order is referred to as either a stop or a lack of stop. The necessary procedures for utilizing this kind of order will be addressed later in more depth.

Stop commands are not necessarily an absolute promise of having particular points of entry or exit. Your broker may only be willing to practically conduct the stop order at values lower or higher than initially anticipated when there are abrupt market fluctuations.

In relation to implementing stop orders for your trader, it is necessary to read and appreciate the relevant instructions. This can eventually affect how you employ them in your trading strategy.

Main Lesson: To further ensure that to minimize each exchange's possible danger, the stop order should be used in practice. Revenues are obtained before pattern reversals or as an essential method.

When a trade goes long, placing a stop loss below an entry point would help guarantee that if a scenario happens where the market reverses, losses are held to the very minimum. In a brief market example, the reverse can be done.

Trading Technique: The precise positions for stop order placing would depend on the trading strategy used. It is worth understanding that if the stop order is placed too close to an entry-stage, then minor price oscillations will contribute to the premature termination of a trade. Therefore, putting stop orders only below or above meaningful amounts of help or opposition is appropriate.

Trailing Stop

A particular form of a stop order, which changes in response to market volatility, is the trailing stop.

A trailing stop changes according to a given trade's path, monitoring a currency's price. The outcome creates a stop level that continuously varies in relation to market fluctuations so that the point at which a trade will close is changed. This tends to lock-in income, and should the price suffer a turnaround, immediately reduce any losses that might arise.

Main Lesson: A vital technique for Forex traders is the trailing stop order, which should be an integral part of many trading strategies.

Trading strategy: If you want to go on the GBP/USD for an extended period and purchase for 1.5780, you should put a trailing stop at 20 pips (initially 1.5760). This would mean that if the price shifts against you and falls through the value of 1.5760, the stop will be enabled and the trade closed.

However, if the price increases, as you have expected, then this value can be monitored and increased appropriately by the trailing stop. If the price manages to hit 1.5800, the trailing stop will now be placed at 20 pips below this current stage, i.e., 1.5780. The stop amount would begin to grow proportionally to represent any price changes. If the currency price continues to decline at some point, then the trailing stop does not fall back but persists at whatever level it hit before the turnaround, in this case, 1.5780.

Since the market does not shift against you by more than 20 pips, the exchange will stay available, at which stage the trade will be locked.

The net effect is that locked-in is the bulk of profits accumulated through the exchange.

Other Order Types

There is a range of more unusual order groups that are more appropriate for seasoned traders, in addition to the four major order types. It could be that these unique order forms never need to be seen, but it may be beneficial to be conscious of them. **They include** well-Until Cancelled (GTC), Good-for-the-Day (GTD); One-The-Other-Cancels (OCO); One The-Other-Triggers (OTO).

Placing an Order

The exact protocol to adopt can differ slightly across brokers and multiple trading platforms after making an order. However, regardless of the particular process, you will need to recognize a variety of common considerations that will shape the base of your trading strategy if you place an order: -

Pick the currency pair that you would like to exchange.

- Determine if the exchange goes long or fast.

-Check the analysis to make sure you are confident about where the price may be heading.

- Review metrics and instruments to improve the plan.

- Predetermine points of exit (using support and resistance).

-Predetermine an aim for the benefit (do not get greedy!).

- Pick a form of order.

- Pick the size of the lot.

- Control the danger relevant to trading (this will be discussed in more detail in later sections). You should either use this or a related checklist before creating any purchases.

It can help plan how you perform transactions and help avoid errors by working through each stage methodically. It acts as a set of checks and balances to evaluate each exchange before making any commitments from various viewpoints.

If an order has been executed, monitoring the trade is essential Tools that can help assess the cumulative performance and incorporate them.

Effective

A Forex trader needs to hold a level mind to try not to act so much on impulse.

Main Lesson

Sticking to a plan is crucial. Sometimes, you can meet your sales goal and believe you can earn profits by remaining in the trade. Chasing gains may be risky because it can raise the risk of getting struck by market reversals by keeping in a trade longer than expected. These risks may be minimized by carefully watching trades and establishing stop losses at suitable thresholds.

In loss-making trades, similar circumstances will exist where it can be enticing to continue with a deal in the expectation that it may inevitably reverse. Set the failure to a halt and stay with it. Losses are a part of life for daily Forex traders, but it would guarantee that you gain more often than you lose by ensuring that they are held to an absolute minimum over time.

Long and Short Positions

The ability to earn money when markets go up or down is one of the Forex industry's most enticing aspects. This ensures that as an investor, pips may be collected regardless of whether they come from upward or downward patterns, significantly raising the available future returns and offering considerable stability in producing a trading strategy.

If the exchange is focused on a transaction where the investor expects that a currency's price would rise over the course of a currency, this is regarded as a long position or going long. On the other side, if the seller allows a deal assuming that the price will decline for sale, this is referred to as a short position or going short.

Why should one Trade Forex?

In every market condition or phase of the business cycle, the cash/spot FOREX markets exhibit specific unique features that give unbeatable prospects for profitable trading. Does this leave one wondering why they care? The response to this is straightforward. It glorifies:

A 24-hour industry (due to the global nature of the Forex market (F.X.), no matter what time during the day or night, you can buy and sell around the clock):

A trader can benefit from all the profitable market conditions at any time, meaning that there is no wait time for the 'opening faceoff' like the exchange.

Greatest liquidity

The most liquid market in the world is the FOREX market. This implies that a trader can join or leave the market whenever they want to have minimum execution obstacles or threats and no daily trading restriction during almost any market condition.

Increased leverage

When contrasted to a leverage ratio of 2 (50 percent margin requirement) in the equity markets, one of up to 400 is standard. This, of course, makes trading an uncomfortable rise in the cash/spot forex market since it tends to make the significant downside loss risk much larger in the same way. It allows the profit opportunity much more impressive on the positive side.

Reduced transaction cost

Under normal market conditions, the retail trading fees (the bid/ask rise) is usually less than 0.1 percent (10 pips). The expansion could be less than five pips at bigger dealers and may significantly increase in rapidly moving markets.

Always a bull market

FOREX market trading means selling or purchasing one currency against the other. In contexts of the worldview for value against other currencies, a bull market or bear market for a currency is described. You get a bull market where a trader makes a profit by purchasing the currency against other currencies if the outcome is positive. However, we have a bull market for other currencies if the outlook is negative, and a trader's profits are forced to sell the currency against any other currency. There is always a bull market exchange chance for a trader in either event.

Inter-bank market

The FOREX market is based on a worldwide network of dealers who communicate and trade via electronic networks and telephones with their customers. There are no organized exchanges like in futures that are there to fulfill as a centralized location to facilitate transactions. This is the way the New York Stock Exchange performs the equity markets

The FOREX market works a lot like the way the NASDAQ market functions in the U.S. It is linked to as an over-the-counter or OTC market just because of that.

No one can dominate the market: the FOREX market is massive and has so many players that no sole company, not even a central bank, can regulate the market price for a longer time.

Even as powerful central banks carry out interventions, they are becoming mostly ineffective and short-lived. This implies that central banks are becoming less and less reluctant to deceive market prices by intervening.

It is unregulated

The FOREX market can be seen as an unregulated industry, although banking regulations restrict primary dealers' activities such as commercial banks in money centers.

Day-to-day FOREX retail brokerage processes are not governed by any rules or policies particular to the FOREX market. Many of these businesses in the United States do not even document to the Internal Revenue Service.

The regulations regulate money futures and options currently traded on exchanges such as the Chicago Mercantile Exchange (CME) to regulate other exchange-traded derivatives. Rather than futures or stocks, there are many distinct benefits to forex trading, such as:

Free Place to Market

With an estimated average of US$1.4 trillion, foreign exchange may be the world's biggest market. That's 46 times as big as all of the futures markets put together! It is complicated for organizations to control their currency's price, with many individuals trading Forex around the world.

Forex trading is simply an excellent alternative to trading futures and commodities. Unless you are a broker, to better guarantee that your project is useful, you will probably want to get some help in forex trading. There are always some risks associated, as with all trading, but if you obey this detailed guide to successful forex trading, the entire process should be much more straightforward. Let's start now!

Rollover of Positions

When the futures contract ends, you must prepare in advance if you are heading to rollover your trades. Every two days, Forex positions expire, and you will need to roll over each trade so that you can remain in your position.

Limited Risk and Ensured Stops

Your risk can be limitless when you are trading futures. For instance, if you assumed Live Cattle prices would have to continue their accelerating trend in December 2003, just before the Mad Cow Infection exploration was discovered in U.S. cattle.

The value for it dropped significantly, which switched the limit down a few days in a row. You would not have been able to leave your place, and as a consequence, this could have flushed out all the savings in your account. You would have been compelled to find even more cash to make up the shortfall in your account as the price just kept falling.

No Commission and No Fees for Exchange

You must pay exchange and brokerage charges when you trade in futures. Forex trading has the benefit of being commission-free. For you, this is far safer. Currency trading is an inter-bank global market that allows buyers to meet sellers in a moment.

Although a broker does not have to pay a service charge to match the purchaser with the salesperson, the rise is usually more significant than when you trade futures.

Suppose you are trading a Japanese Yen/U.S. Dollar pair, for instance, forex trading, would have a spread of about 3 points (worth $30). Trading a J.Y. markets trade would most probably have a 1 point spread (worth $10), but you would also be fined the broker's fee on top of that. This price could be as low for self-directed online trading as $11 in-and-out or as high for full-service trading as $100. However, all-inclusive pricing is included.

To see which commission is the largest, you will have to try comparing both internet forex and your particular futures commission charge.

Lower Margin

A forex trader has the authority to influence a substantial amount of the currency essentially by putting up a fair portion of percentage, just like futures and stock speculation.

However, futures trading's margin requirements are generally around 5 percent of the holding's full value, or 50 percent of a stock's total price. The forex margin requirements are about 1 percent. For instance, the margin needed for foreign exchange trading is $1000 for every $100,000.

This implies that a currency trader's money, trading forex, can carry five times as much production value as a futures trader's, or 50 times more than a stock trader's.

This can be a very financially viable method to develop an investment strategy when trying to trade on percentage. Still, you must try to understand the dangers that are also implicated.

You should make sure you understand completely how your bridge loan is going to function. You will want to make sure that you read the margin pact for both you and your cleaning company. If you have any queries, you will also want to speak with your accounting manager.

On the possibility that the accessible margin in your account falls below a set amount, the locations you have in your account could be partially or fully liquidated.

Before your positions are liquidated, you may not get a margin call. Because of this, daily, you should evaluate your margin balance and use stop-loss orders to restrict downside risk in every available spot.

When is the Forex Market Open?

For futures, you are generally restricted to dealing only during the few hours in which each market is open for one day. When the banks are closed, if a big news event comes out, you would not have a way to buy out of it until the market reopens, which may be several hours away.

Forex, on the other side, is a business that's 24/5. In New York, the day starts and leads the sun across the globe across Europe, Asia, Australia, and then to the U.S. You can trade from Monday to Friday any time you want.

In the Forex Market, What Do We Trade?

In the forex sector, we exchange currency. Forex trade does not occur in an over-the-counter (OTC) market but directly between two entities, unlike shares or securities. A global network of banks operates the forex sector, distributed across four main forex trading centers in various geographical locations: New York, London, Sydney, and Tokyo. You can exchange Forex 24 hours a day because there is no central spot.

Three distinct types of forex market:

Spot forex market: a currency pair's physical trading that takes place at the same moment where the transaction is completed, i.e., 'on the spot' or during a limited amount of time.

Forward forex market: a deal is reached to purchase or sell a fixed quantity of a currency at a given price, to be decided in the future or within the future several times at a specified date.

Future forex market: a deal is negotiated to acquire or sell, at a fixed price and time in the future, a certain sum of a specified currency. A futures deal is legally valid; unlike forwards, many traders speculating on forex markets do not expect to take possession of the currency itself; instead, they create projections on exchange rates to take advantage of market price fluctuations.

How do you Trade Forex?

It may seem overwhelming to understand how to trade as in any other market, so we've subdivided forex trading into some easy steps to help you get started:

- Decide how you'd like to trade Forex

- Learn how the forex market works

- Open an account

- Build a trading plan

- Choose your forex trading platform

- Open, monitor, and close your first position

Determine how you'd like to trade Forex

There is a lot of forex trade among global banks and financial institutions, who purchase large currency quantities per day. However, there are two fundamental methods of getting interested in individual traders who may not have the resources to create billion-dollar forex trades: forex CFDs or selling Forex with a broker.

What is a CFD forex?

A forex CFD is a deal in which you choose to swap a money pair's price differential from when you start up your position till when you shut it. Open up a long bet, and you'll make a return if the forex position rises in volume. You will make a loss if it decreases in cost. Open up a brief role, and the reverse is true. Forex is only one of the markets where you can use CFDs for trade.

CHAPTER 2: Trading Forex through a Broker

Forex trading through a broker operates in a fairly similar fashion to CFD trading, or often via a fund. You are speculating about currency pairs' market fluctuations without necessarily having control of the currencies themselves. If you think the price of a currency pair is heading downwards rather than long, you should go short. However, while you exchange Forex via a dealer, you would not have links to other markets.

Check out how the forex industry performs:

How a forex market works is among the first things to understand whether you begin to swap currencies and is somewhat different from exchange-based schemes such as bonds or futures.

Forex is purchased and sold through a bank network rather than buying and selling currency on a centralized market. This is named as the market for over-the-counter, or OTC. It works because these banks, providing a bid price to purchase a specific currency pair and a quoted price to sell a forex pair, function like market makers.

Trading through forex providers

Many retail traders would not purchase and sell Forex directly from one of the financial institutions, utilizing a forex trading provider. Forex exchange providers negotiate on your side with the banks, seeking the best deals possible and contributing to their business spread.

Some companies would encourage you to communicate with order books from market makers directly. This is defined as direct market access, or DMA, which suggests that without the spread, advanced traders will

Buy and sell Forex rather than selling at the rates provided by currency sellers, plus an adjustable reward.

Opening an Account

You would need an account with a diversified trading provider if you would like to exchange Forex via CFDs. You can launch an I.G. account in mines, and until you want to position a trade, there's no requirement to include funding.

Build a trading strategy

It's essential to develop a trading strategy if you're new to the markets. A trading strategy helps take the decision-making feeling because it offers some stability as you open and close your positions. You will also want to start utilizing a forex trading strategy that controls how you locate market opportunities.

It's time to implement it after you have selected a specific forex trading approach. In the markets you choose to sell, use your favorite technical forecasting methods to determine your first trade.

You should also pay heed to any changes that seem likely to trigger uncertainty, even though you prefer to be a strictly technical investor. For example, future economic reports might well resonate through the forex markets, which your technical research does not take into consideration.

Choose your forex trading platform:

Trading platforms can support a smart and more comfortable way to exchange Forex. You may trade-in:

- Online using your choice of web browser

- Or using a mobile application

- You may also use advanced third parties channels such as MT4

Each of these forex trading (F.X.) platforms, with customized updates, interactive maps, and risk management software, can be customized to match your trading needs and personality.

Open, monitor, and close your first position:

You will begin trading after you have selected a platform. Only open the offer ticket for the selected area, then you'll see both the buying price and the selling price mentioned. You will also be allowed to determine your place's scale and introduce some limits or restrictions until it reaches a certain amount that will shut your exchange. To start a long position or sold to open a short position, press purchase.

In the 'available positions' segment of the dealing forum, you will track your position's benefit/loss. Once you've agreed that it's time to close your place when you open it, just make the opposite trade.

2.1   The Brokers' role

You have to remember quite a few items first when it comes to getting involved with forex trading. The first thing you ought to do is locate and select the best broker, which involves choosing a business that fits your unique criteria to support you make your trades.

When selecting a broker, you need to realize that much as in every other market and several FOREX brokers to choose from. In making your decision, there are a few aspects that you need to check for:

Different Types of Account

Your brokerage business can have an account as a Forex novice. It has all the required resources for researching, knowing, and practicing trade strategies. It should also have an account to enable you to make trades that are appropriate for your budget.

You may be given two or three forms of accounts by certain brokers. The smallest account is referred to as a mini account, which allows you to exchange for at least $300.

This allows you a strong degree of control (required to profit with a small initial capital). The basic account helps you to exchange at several various leverages, but to get you off, it often needs a fixed initial capital of $2,000.

Finally, to get you off, there are premium accounts, which also need large sums of cash. It often requires varying levels of leverage to be utilized and also provides additional instruments and facilities.

You would need to guarantee that the broker you chose provides the proper leverage, instruments, and resources that apply to the amount of money you can operate.

A Variety of Leverage Options

In FOREX dealing, leverage is a crucial requirement since the market fluctuations (the origins of revenue) are set at bare percentages of a quarter. Leverage, represented as a percentage of gross leverage accessible to real capital, is the sum of money a trader will loan you for selling.

For starters, if you have a 100:1 ratio, this implies your broker would loan you $100 for every $1 in real cash. You can be provided as much as 250:1 by several brokerage agencies.

Of course, you need to note that reduced debt still implies a lower chance of a margin call, but it also means that your buck can get a lower knock

(And vice versa). Practically, you ought to know that your broker has high leverage if you have few resources.

If capital is not a concern, you should be confident that it should be enough for any broker with a broad range of leverage choices. A selection of choices helps you to adjust the level of difficulty you are prepared to accept. For, e.g., while you are dealing with too unpredictable (exotic) currency pairs, less leverage (and thus less risk) could be advantageous.

Extensive Analysis and Tools

Just as traders in other industries do, FOREX brokers provide several various trading channels for their customers. Real-time maps, technical research software, real-time news and statistics, and even aid for the different trading networks are also seen on these various trading platforms.

You would need to make sure to order free trials before agreeing to any one broker in particular so that you can try their numerous trading platforms.

As a way of aiding you, brokers typically have technological and basic remarks, financial calendars, and other studies. You're going to want to locate a broker that offers you everything you need to thrive.

Low Spreads

Spread, measured in pips, is the disparity between the price at which currency can be acquired and the price at which currency can be exchanged at any given moment. FOREX dealers do not pay a fee because this distinction is how they are going to earn profits.

You can find that the gap between spreads in FOREX is as big as the gap in profits in the stock arena while you are contrasting brokers. This implies that lower spreads can save you cash, so search for a low spread broker.

Quality of the Institution

Unlike stockbrokers, because of the vast sums of capital needed, FOREX brokers are typically connected to large banks or lending institutions.

FOREX brokers should also be licensed with the Merchant of the Futures Commission (FCM) and controlled by the Commodity Futures Trading Commission (CFTC).

This and other financial reports and figures regarding a FOREX brokerage can be contained on the company's website or its parent company's website. You'll want to make sure that a reputable organization helps your broker.

2.2 Broker Types

Two major categories of Forex brokers provide retail traders with entry to the marketplace: Market Makers - who decide and set their bids and ask for rates.

Electronic Communications Networks (ECN) - which use the most substantial bid and offer rates accessible from interbank institutions? A commercial pop forex provider will provide the perfect option for most retail traders with tools suitable for both newbies and those with growing experience levels.

Brokers, You Ought to Avoid

Just like the brokers you want, there are brokers you want to stay away from too. For starters, brokers who are likely to purchase or sell predetermined close points unnecessarily (frequently known as sniping and hunting) are trifling things done by brokers who only aim to maximize income.

No broker will necessarily confess to doing this, certainly, but there are ways to tell if a broker perpetrated this crime.

Sadly, talking to fellow traders is the only way you will decide which brokers do it and which brokers don't. No actual registry or agency is documenting this operation of this kind. The argument here is that to locate out that is an honest broker. You have to speak in person with others or attend internet discussion forums.

Strict Margin Rules

Your broker should have a right to take part in how much danger you can take when trading with borrowed funds. Your broker will purchase or sell at his or her option with this insight, which can be a feeble thing for you.

Let's just say that you have a margin account, and before it starts to recover to all-time highs, your position takes a headlong downward turn. Even if you have enough capital to support it, your place on a margin call at that low would be liquidated by certain brokers. This behavior will cost you dearly on their side. To find out who the truthful traders are, you chat in person with someone or join online conversation boards.

It's a lot like having an equity account to subscribe to a FOREX transaction. The one significant distinction is that you are expected to sign a margin arrangement on FOREX accounts.

Practically, this deal specifies that you are selling borrowed capital, and because of this, the investment company can intervene with the transactions to preserve its interests. All you have to do after you sign up is finance your account, and you'll be able to exchange right away.

2.3 Benefits and Drawbacks of Employing Forex Brokers

You probably know when it comes to Forex trading that most traders use brokers to accomplish their trades. Your broker controls your online financial account, allowing you to sell. Therefore they are a crucial component of the exchange.

With the number of traders conned by brokers growing, you have to be cautious while choosing one. Not only does the correct broker make your trading more comfortable, but also more profitable.

Cost friendly

Because of their commissions, one explanation why specific traders dislike brokers is. However, despite any proportion of the earnings being taken over by the dealers, their reduction is negligible.

Their prices are very fair considering the nature of the services they provide. In addition to the percentage, brokers will also take your spread with a sum of currency.

Nevertheless, their decrease is even smaller relative to other online financial transfers from various sectors.

Access to Practice/Demo Accounts

Before you start trading for real, most brokerage websites offer you either a small sum of money or unlimited funds to play around. Without risking thousands of dollars in savings, this helps you feel for the markets and better appreciate whether forex trading is correct for you.

Restrictions by financial institutions

Major financial organizations around the globe also govern the most respectable brokers. Such entities are all regulated by numerous rules.

Although the laws regulating multiple brokers may vary, all of them serve a single function, shielding traders from fraud. Your broker will help you figure things out if you find an issue with your trading site.

The laws regulating brokers often discourage them from cheating you off. They should, therefore, not be interested in criminal tasks such as market price-fixing.

You can be confident that your hard-earned money is secure, as long as your broker is monitored.

Access to platforms for trading

In addition to clarity, brokers can provide you with links to the market's strongest online trading sites. Different platforms offer numerous features and functionalities, and therefore it would cost you enormously to pick the wrong one.

Your broker knows the techniques and types of trading and thus chooses the right medium for you.

Responsiveness, efficiency, and ease of navigation are a few aspects that make a successful trading platform. Besides, trading sites have helpful features, such as resources for technical research.

Your Forex trading broker can link you to a platform appropriate for your level based on your level of experience.

Transparency

You probably want to know how the trade activities shift anywhere your money is concerned. These details should be given to you by your broker. Transparency enables you to make meaningful financial choices that could benefit your trade. Moreover, without altering the sector, the regulation requires controlled brokers to be fully honest with their customers. Hence, you can be assured of secure, fair trading by hiring a broker. Look into their previous accounting records to stop a bogus broker. Brokers who do not have this study are creating a big red flag.

Disadvantages

Fees

About any trade you create on a forex market, from financing your account to exchanging currency to removing currencies back into a bank account, has fees associated with it. Ultimately, forex traders are corporations, and they aim to preserve their bottom line.

Often, how they want to remain in business is by wise tactics that ensure that their consumers retain some of their profits, but others skim off the top even more than required. It is crucial for forex trading to ensure that the fees concerning your broker are known.

Scam Risk

Some brokers will gladly take your capital, but they will be far more reluctant to offer it back to you. Many brokers either have confusing terms and conditions designed to confuse and suppress your attempts to withdraw your cash or are blatant fraud that only becomes evident after you have attempted to withdraw.

Some brokers have extraordinarily high minimum withdrawal conditions that render it difficult for most traders to extract the cashback into their possession.

A decent forex broker would represent the best interests and maintain the service while keeping a meager portion for them. On the other side, poor forex traders would defraud you everywhere they can get at any switch and penny-pinch. Before subscribing to every forex trader, make sure to research them before committing extensively. Do your utmost to explore non-biased forex trading data outlets such as business24-7 so that you are not only fed ads veiled as genuine ratings.

2.4 How do forex brokers earn?

Most people don't care about how traders earn their profits while dealing with Forex. Before depositing, though, there is a fundamental point to consider, and you can understand that money moves in the scheme. Nobody worries more than you do for your account, so bear that in mind while finding out whom you want to trust. We'll look at how Forex brokers make money in this segment and their position in liquidity facilitation.

Understanding how Forex traders make money will help you pick the best broker. Some brokers have a handful of commissions they use to benefit from their buyers. Being acquainted with these solutions can help you appreciate where your cash is headed. The primary source of earning is broker fees.

Certain Forex traders pay a fee per transaction, while others charge the spread between the bid/ask rates. The primary way Forex brokers earn money is by maintaining the spread of charging a fixed fee per round switch. Few brokers also charge both, although these days, as the market's commoditization needs lower prices, that's becoming less popular.

Unfortunately, some less than scrupulous Forex traders have previously claimed that they have free trading commissions, but what they usually do is demand enough to make up the gap in the spread.

The distribution is often constant, often variable. The sum of the spread would focus on how many orders are out there in a variable spread liquidity pool. The spread would usually expand anytime there is a bug report, such as the Nonfarm Payroll Figures coming out of the United States. Because of this, you might end up spending more than you plan in a competitive market. This is the most significant value of a fixed spread, so at least you'll realize what you're going to be paying and make things easy to purchase and sell.

Alternate revenue streams

When it comes to customer support and schooling, specific Forex traders can charge extra for' bells and whistles'. For example, for those who can pay extra or provide a more comprehensive plan, some will provide signals, some will provide in-depth research, and some may also offer private educational classes and webinars. That being said, these things are very rarely needed if you understand trading and proper money management techniques.

Paying the "loan" is another means that individual Forex traders can earn profits. Know, you are taking out a loan anytime you purchase or short a currency with a margin. This can get a little confusing and dicey, but it's enough to tell the F.X.

In the actual interbank market, traders with vast volumes of orders will get charged interest, something of which you would not engage. About what people say you, you don't get anywhere near the actual Interbank market as a retail trader, so orders need to be far more significant to succeed in that arena.

The Forex broker would usually deal with the liquidity supplier that shops these orders in smaller bits, enabling individuals to exchange back and forth.

The actual interbank market comprises the world's biggest banks that cannot be troubled by a minor exchange worth $500 (for example).

CHAPTER 3: Trade Mechanics

Trading currency is a method of swapping one currency for another because two transactions coincide with any currency exchange. While the other is exchanged, one currency is acquired. As currency pairs, the forex market quotes values to promote the convenience of exchanging one currency with another.

A currency pair quotation reflects the number of units of one currency needed to buy or sell the other currency pair's equal sum, depending on the question's exchange rate.

For instance, if the exchange rate between the U.S. dollar and the Canadian dollar is $1.12, for a single U.S. dollar, a dealer can purchase 1.12 Canadian dollars, or buy one dollar for every 1.12 Canadian dollars.

As a currency dealer, the aim is to keep the currency you think would gain value against the other quoted in the pair. It's genuinely as plain as that.

3.1   Currency Pairs

Every currency pair consists of two parts: the base currency and the currency of the quotation. The example of the U.S. dollar/Canadian dollar we just mentioned is paired as USD/CAD, for instance. The base currency is always on the left side of the slash (/) mark; the currency quoted is still on the slash's right side. It is the base currency position that you weigh to determine whether to purchase or sell a currency pair.

If you assume that the base currency would appreciate against the currency quoted, the currency pair will be bought. If you consider that the base currency would depreciate against the currency quoted, the pair of currencies will be sold. For novice traders, this is an essential difference to note that it is simple to purchase by mistake when you wish to sell. Currency pairs sold on the forex market are designed utilizing both established and emerging market currencies.

The exchange rate defined by the currency pair implies that the base currency gives the basis of all transactions. Therefore, if you were to put a GBP/USD (British pound/U.S. dollar) purchasing order, you will purchase the base currency (GBP) while selling the quotation currency at the same time (USD). Conversely, you would sell the base currency (GBP) while purchasing the quote currency if you were to sell the same pair (USD).

Main lesson: You would purchase the currency pair to create a lucrative exchange, if you felt that the base currency would increase or improve in value, or if you expected the base currency to depreciate or decrease in value relative to the quote currency over the period, you will sell the currency pair.

3.2 Major Pairs

The most liquid and heavily traded currency pairs on the forex market are from countries with highly developed economies and financial systems like: the euro, the U.S. dollar, the British pound, the Swiss franc, the Japanese yen, the Australian dollar, and the Canadian dollar are among the main currencies.

3.3 Cross-Pairs (Minor Pair)

Some currencies are not cited against each other directly; however, by mixing two separate pairs, they are synthetically exchanged. Currency pairs like GBP/JPY, EUR/JPY, EUR/CHF, and GBP/CHF are used in these pairs, classified as cross-pairs.

The deal is truly constructed by purchasing GBP/USD and selling USD/JPY while a dealer conducts a transaction to buy GBP/JPY. The dollar part of this exchange is equivalent, and long GBP and short JPY end up with the dealer.

Since these pairs are designed with two distinct currency pairs, a cross-spread pair's or cost of exchange is considerably greater than a standard central currency pair, such as EUR/USD.

Liquidity of Currencies

It is necessary to recognize that two main factors drive the exchange rate between two currencies until we pass on to exotic currencies: natural supply and demand. The relationship between those two currencies and other currencies, most prominently the USD.

If you swap GBP for EUR, all importers and exporters in the U.K. can exchange GBP for EUR. And Europe is going to purchase and sell all currencies and have an active demand.

If you swap GBP for NZD, on the other side, there would be fewer importers and market-active exporters-the quotations are more likely to be a mix of the GBPUSD rate and the USDNZD rate.

Exchanging one currency for another for currencies that are much less liquid would eventually entail exchanging the first currency for USD and then exchanging USD for the second currency.

Many forex brokers provide forex trading to clients either in the direct currency sector or via CFDs (contracts for difference). Either way, the spreads they deliver rely on the underlying currency market's liquidity.

Although you can see a pair quoted as only two currencies, a market maker may have to perform an additional leg at any stage for the transactions to take place in the underlying market.

3.4　Exotic Pairs of Currencies

In comparison to a lightly exchanged currency or an emerging-market.

Economic currency, exotic pairs usually comprise a major currency.

USD/TRY, USD/MXN, or EUR/HUF is instances.

An advantage of exotic trading pairs is that they can give higher potential returns due to large market variations. This suggests, however, that they are more dangerous to trade.

Although there are over 150 nations that may be listed as emerging nations, 18 currencies are exotic currency trade. For starters, Admiral Markets U.K. Ltd, a popular forex and CFD broker, lists 19 exotic F.X. Pairs of currencies, like ten tropical currencies. There are tons of other exotic currencies, but brokers can only sell their buyers' demands in most situations.

The most commonly exchanged tropical currencies include the following:

- Czech Koruna
- Polish Zloty
- Norwegian Krone
- Russian Ruble

- Hungarian Forint

- Chinese Yuan Rimini

- Turkish Lira

- Hong Kong Dollar

- Singaporean Dollar

- Thai Baht

- South Korean Won

- Indonesian Rupiah

- Malay Ringgit

- Mexican Peso

- Indian Rupee

- South African Rand

- Brazilian Real

The spreads provided for a currency pair would represent the underlying liquidity for that pair with every broker. E.g., Admiral Markets provides spreads as low as 0.1 pips for the EURUSD pair (the world's most liquid pair) to 5 pips for CADCHF and 10 pips for USDCNH. Spreads can be much wider for even less liquid currencies, reaching 800 pips in some cases.

3.5   Platforms for Forex trading

Trading in Forex (F.X.) is done electronically using an electronic trading platform. Many traders are naturally concerned about what is the strongest trading Forex site. Which Forex trading platform is, in reality, the best? One of the biggest questions a trader raises at the outset of their trading trip is' this is very valid in modern days when tech has many rivalries out there.

There are several different kinds of Forex trading sites since each trader creates their specialized tools. This helps them select the functionality, style, and services supported by their website. It is not clear to grasp a Forex network and how it functions. Often Forex traders can focus a judgment about how it appears and smells, but you need to know what is under the bonnet, like a vehicle.

You may create an account on many types of online FOREX trading sites, so here's a short rundown of the various categories of platforms and how they vary.

Downloadable vs. Non-downloadable sites for trading

The first factor for the classification of forex trading sites is whether they can or cannot be downloaded. Downloadable trading sites are more or fewer programs (or software) that can only be viewed and configured on the individual computer on which they have been installed (this may be a mobile device or a computer).

Platforms that are not downloadable are web-based and can be used on any computer that has internet connectivity. What you need is to open the page and enter the information of your log-in.

When selecting a downloadable or cloud-based application (bear in mind that specific applications can only work on local computers, they are built on, i.e., FOREX trading software installed on P.C.), it is a question of discretion as to how and where you transact (accessibility should be the primary concern alongside functionality requirements).

3.6   MetaQuotes Platforms

As it comes to F.X. investing. Most brokers can provide you with different trading platforms online, but MetaTrader platforms are the most popular. This app was built about ten years ago.

There are two major alternatives currently provided by MetaQuotes Corp

- MetaTrader 4 and MetaTrader 5 - for the trading site.

3.7   MetaTrader 4

MetaTrader 4 is a tool that has been built exclusively for F.X. For trade.

As retail Forex is a relatively young business, before MetaTrader 4 emerged, it did not have credible third-party applications enabled. This is a reliable trading platform that offers lots of useful features for traders.

They include:

- Trading by 1-click
- Lots of expert advisors are available
- Over 50 benchmarks
- Orders waiting
- Restrict orders
- Multi-diagramming
- Nine separate timeframes

Benefits of MetaTrader 4

Those are only a handful of MetaTrader 4's advantages. Its stability is one of its most vital selling points. You can rely on this network, truly. It is also equipped with a versatile collection of smartphone applications in addition to this. These applications are available for almost every form of the operating system, like Android and Windows. These mobile platforms are also very reliable and strong.

3.8   The MetaTrader 5

This is very close to MetaTrader 4, one of the most robust forex trading services accessible at the moment. MetaTrader 5 is usually marginally quicker, accepts more orders, comes with a more remarkable set of metrics, and has several extra functions.

There are no significant, groundbreaking variations that can render MetaTrader 4 obsolete, even if it is a better tool. What's interesting about MetaTrader 5 for both traders and brokers is that, relative to MetaTrader 4, it can accommodate a fantastic range of trading instruments.

Benefits of MetaTrader 5

Several distinct benefits are not present in other forex trading sites, though MetaTrader 5 is comparable to MetaTrader 4.

MetaTrader 5, for instance, has:

- 21 timeframes that can be interpreted by the trader.

- It comprises 11 kinds of 'minute' charts (such as M1, M2, M3,....), seven types of 'hourly charts (such as H1, H2, H3,... and regular, weekly, and monthly charts.

- Many platforms come with just nine timeframes, such as MetaTrader 4.

- Six forms of pending requests, including purchase-stop, sell-stop, purchase-limit, sell-limit, purchase-stop-limit, and sell-stop-limit.

- Usually, MetaTrader 4 and other platforms deliver the first four categories of pending orders only.

- The opportunity to move between mode 'hedging' and mode' netting.

- Hedging mode provides the right to take trades in competing positions, which has revolutionized Forex traders' trading options.

- The Depth of Demand (DOM) feature enables Forex traders to display a financial instrument's bids and offers at various rates.

3.9 CTrader

Spotware has developed 'cTrader' as a rival trading site for Forex traders in recent years. While the platform provides advanced charting and trading functionality, there are several variants close to the MetaTrader platform:

Since MetaTrarevolutionized the best-known auto-trading sites, it has a broad online community discussing new tactics and indicators. It also allows it much simpler to find support for MetaTrader platforms on the internet, while support for the auto-trading features of cTrader can be minimal.

CTrader does not enable indicator customization and has restrictions on third parties' usage, while MetaTrader is entirely customizable.

MetaTrader comes bundled with extra functionality, such as an economic calendar, business news in real-time, and signal trading tools, although cTrader does not have all of these functions.

As this platform is accessible in a web browser, there has not been a heavy focus on creating smartphone applications recently. CTrader is currently only supported for Android and its users. Although this possibly protects most merchants, those using a Windows phone are hampered by it. For Forex smartphone trading, MetaTrader 4 and 5 are the most important trading sites.

CHAPTER 4: Trends

You're sure to have used the expression, 'your friend is the trend,' which is a precious reminder to note. It is essential to consider the market trends you invest in utilizing the different trading strategies mentioned in this book.

In various conditions, this can help you determine which method you can apply. For instance, Fibonacci can effectively be extended to pattern prices, whereas pivot points and thresholds of support/resistance are better adapted in various markets.

A trending market is one where markets shift in one path primarily. Over this time, there might be brief retracements when rates shift in a different direction for a short period, but the general average trend may continue on the same track. Conversely, rates can vary across various economies, going both up and down without a consistent direction.

Main Lesson: There are sometimes cycles of market movement when no discernable pattern can be apparent, and it is often prudent to try to stop selling at these moments as a Forex novice.

As markets vary and when there is just sideways activity in the sector, more seasoned traders can find gains, although these cycles may historically produce false signals, and the uncertainty at these moments can result in volatile price fluctuations.

As you acquire more insight and awareness of tactics applicable under various situations, you can continue to take advantage of these possibilities. You may split down market trends into three main groups: upward trend, downward trend, or oscillating/ranging.

4.1 The Upward Trend

As more customers are involved in the market than sellers, an upward pattern emerges because prices increase over time. Using technical analysis makes it easy to merely detect an upward trend by linking the lower troughs in the market action. They will shape a simple upward curving trend line when they are related, reinforcing the ongoing movement in an upward trend.

Main Lesson: A basic rule when drawing trend lines is that for it to be used as a valid predictor, you should be able to link at least three points on the graph.

4.2 Downward Trend

As there are more sellers of a specific currency than buyers, downward patterns emerge, leading to a price drop across the era. By linking a sequence of increasingly lower peaks or highs in the market movement, technical analysis to define a downward pattern is accomplished. A set of 3 touchpoints is needed to draw a consistent downward trend line.

4.3 Oscillation (Ranging)

The market is oscillating or ranging where there is no easily discernible pattern apparent in the price fluctuations. There are fluctuations in market volatility over this time, sometimes between support and opposition levels, when the price varies between the limits of a certain range.

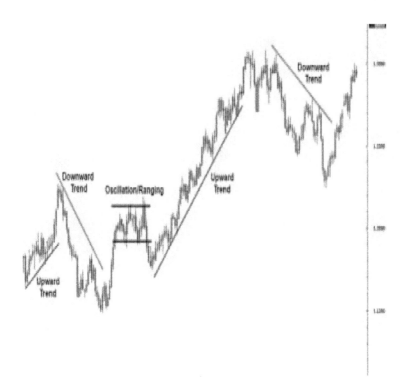

Trend Lines Drawing

Trend lines are one of the easiest technical research methods and can also be highly productive if applied correctly. To reliably plot the latest market trends, should often be the first method of measurement utilized and, whenever possible, paired with other technical analysis techniques.

Drawing clear trend lines involve two big tops or bottoms in price action and then connected. Two touchpoints are sufficient to create a pattern, and then a third is needed to validate the trend. In an upward direction, the line would connect the lower support points (troughs), and the line would link the higher resistance point in a downward trend (peaks).

Drawing Trend Lines

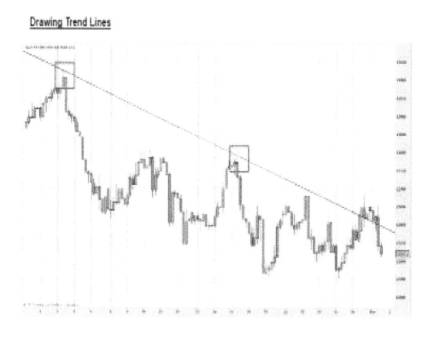

There are three pattern types: Upward, Downward, and Ranging (Sideways). The steeper a pattern, the less reliable it is expected to be, and thus the greater the risk that it will be disrupted. The further points that can be associated along with a graph, the greater the trend's importance.

Main lesson: It is crucial to often draw a trend line based on the available evidence and not to make the error of attempting to match the data to a trend that is interpreted.

Resistance and Support

Resistance and Support are two terms that for technological research are considered to be highly significant. It may be challenging to understand both since there are always different views among traders about how best to measure amounts of Resistance and Support.

When markets are going in a particular direction, there are many occasions when a threshold is hit above which traders can fail to drive prices. Then specific amounts are regarded as resistance because this is used in an upward market trend. They are behaving as a price limit, stopping travel above them.

Alternatively, they are regarded as Support when these thresholds are hit in a decreasing path, and they function like a barrier that keeps prices from falling further.

These levels grow in reaction to consumer behavior and a function of the general attitude in the market. Suppose traders believe a price is going up too fast or being overvalued. In that case, the bulk of the market will oppose this behavior whenever some community of traders tries to drive prices higher than the resistance limit. This indicates that the consumer has determined that it might be too expensive to see a premium above that amount and not accept such rates for that currency.

This lack of appetite ultimately causes resistance. In the case of the service rate, the reverse is true. In this period, if the overriding investor perception is that the price sinks below the value at which most traders believe it should be sold, then help may be said to be there. This suggests that traders favor current values in general and believe that the valuation does not slip below current amounts.

It also ends in the market, rebounding in the opposite direction when the price reaches places of help or resistance. This may occur in either a big reversal of motion or only a minor shift.

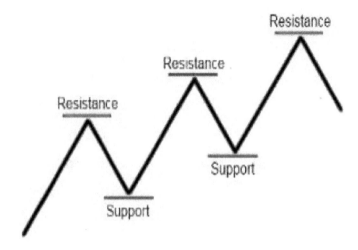

While amounts of Support and opposition serve as price movement barriers, that is not to suggest that they are unbreakable. When traders strive to decide if the price should be higher or lower, markets can sometimes vary between specific amounts of support and resistance over some time.

When an occurrence that starts to drive prices primarily in one direction is to arise, so it is far more probable that either the amount of support or resistance may be broken. When the price effectively breaks through each of these thresholds, it will grow new resistance and help levels, considering these improvements.

As a consequence of these shifts, the degrees of help and opposition can be viewed as complex entities, implying that they are continually re-adjusting and moving in response to market movements. There are several methods to measure these degrees of assistance and resistance, all of which will be explored in later pages.

Support & Resistance

Main Lesson: Help and resistance levels are generally recognized as reliable 'signposts' in places where crime is expected to occur. This suggests that it is realistic to anticipate markets at these amounts to either breakthrough or recover. If one of these incidents happens, it is possible to schedule transactions that can be capitalized.

Pivot Points

Pivot points are one tool that can be used to measure help or resistance thresholds that are critical to signaling a transition in price movement.

They may be used to assess the levels at which a market is expected to reverse or the values to which prices are needed to pass to show real price breakouts. Essentially, pivot points are seen as critical indicators to predict when market shifts can arise and to decide when and where transactions can be conducted as part of trading strategies.

In various forms, pivot points are measured, and usually, this can be achieved automatically using charting tools. A fundamental understanding of the underlying methodology of producing pivot points is essential. The most popular calculation form, which is known as the Five-Point Scheme, is illustrated below: Pivot Point = (High + Low + Close) / 3

First Support = High First Resistance = (Pivot Point x 2) (Pivot Point x 2)

2)-Low Second Support= Pivot Point-(High-Low) Second Resistance= Pivot Point+ (High-Low) Charting tools can be used as graphic representations on currency maps to transpose these values.

Pivot Points

The values for measuring these quantities are typically taken at 4 pm EST as the Forex market runs 24hrs a day. It is necessary to use alternative ways of estimating pivot points, and it might be useful to have an awareness of these other methodologies.

Use Points Pivot

Pivot points are a potent intra-day trading mechanism since they offer good indicators of market support and resistance levels. The key degree of support or opposition is the pivot point itself, and it is at this point, the biggest market change may be predicted to arise. In essence, the price may be expected to either "bounce off the pivot point or "breakthrough it.

Pivot Point - Bounce

Pivot points may be used to assess where patterns are emerging in the industry. This implies the formation of a general downward trend if the price breaks below the pivot point. Equally, when the price breaks above this stage, it will mean the beginning of an upward trend. Therefore, if prices bounce off the pivot point, this implies a stabilization phase when no particular pattern is present.

Because pivot points are focused on the previous day's data, they are just a short-term predictor and must be recalculated regularly. Many charting software does this automatically. Pivot points may also be a valuable method to assess where and when the market can join and leave. The best strategy for doing this depends on the pivot point to signal these degrees of entry and exit.

For starters, if the price breaks below the pivot point, you might use this to join the business as an indicator. To set a stop failure, you will then use the pivot point price (ideally, this should be placed just above this level to prevent your trade being closed early should the price rebound back towards the pivot point at any time). For that specific exchange, the first help level can then be used as the goal price.

If the price starts to move below this first support level, then you could either opt to leave the trade, take your advantage, or use the first support level as its current place to reposition your stop loss.

In this scenario, the benefit goal would now become the second degree of funding. Every trade should be well placed to take advantage of the trending markets by using this strategy and using pivot points to set the different strategic levels while staying safe from any rebounds or reversals in motion.

There are several variables connected with the usage of pivot points that involve a degree of care. It is regularly difficult to assess how the market is behaving at any given moment, and it may be difficult to discern in which direction a potential change might be if the price hovers near the pivot point. Prices will rarely reverse until they hit the amount of help and resistance collection, culminating in a failed technique.

Key lesson: It is necessary, in conjunction with other metrics, to use pivot points and ensure that the overall market pattern is taken into account in the forecast of future movements. Where appropriate, trading against the pattern should be prevented!

Volume

Another critical element of technological research and tracking price volatility is to be conscious of the amount of action taking place in the sector at any given moment, which implies volume comprehension.

Amount simply corresponds to the number of transactions that take place over some time, offering accurate statistics about the number of traders involved, as well as reflecting consumer interest in the acquisition or sale of a given currency.

Many charting tools, at the bottom of each chart, can have volume levels for previous cycles. Much as fluctuations in the real stock price will disclose valuable facts, the study of volume volumes can often assess patterns.

In reality, due to the size and nature of the number of individual trades taking place every day and the absence of a coordinated organization to track this multitude of transactions, there is no real measure of volume in the Forex markets.

Moreover, marketers would be mindful of the average quantities of transactions that exist at any particular moment, and these statistics may be helpful to track.

Each bar in a volume chart would reflect the number of transactions performed in that specific time and show whether there was a higher net number of purchasing or selling orders overall.

It is necessary to note to track volume, as proof of a specific pattern's accuracy would also be assisted where there is an up or down market change that is followed by a reasonably large rate of trading action. Hence, a reliable trend movement is more probable than if volatility levels were slightly smaller.

Key lesson: Technically, this implies that once you have established a certain pattern, by some means, it is necessary to review the volume levels to decide if trading levels accompany your research.

Generally, volume volumes often shift in step with the prevalent pattern.

If a pattern generates traction in a specific direction, a growing scale would also be followed by an increasing scale, indicating a growing number of consumer participants reinforce the trend.

When markets shift to take advantage of the rising or declining pattern, this would eventually drive prices even higher. When traders' enthusiasm for a given pattern continues to decline, this would be followed by a relative reduction in volume volumes, as traders grow suspicious of the underlying trend. This adopting of a more conservative stance appears to signal either a stabilization phase or indicates that there could be an impending pattern reversal.

In addition to promoting the detection of overarching phenomena, the volume may also be a significant consideration when utilizing chart patterns for technical research. In these cases, as complex trends form, the volume becomes a consideration in deciding if the predicted result of the trend is likely to occur and whether other traders endorse the understanding of market conditions.

4.4 Forex Charts

The secret to successful technical analysis maps and there are various ways to view Forex info. Charts to be careful of include: line charts, bar charts, and charts of candlesticks.

Line Chart

The easiest description of currency market fluctuations is line graphs. A constant line is used to link the closing price of the current session to the preceding session's closing price. Therefore the details shown by this sort of chart have little detail, but it may be quite important to display rising and declining patterns across trading sessions.

Main lesson: Line charts are incredibly helpful to indicate general price changes in markets.

Forex Line Chart

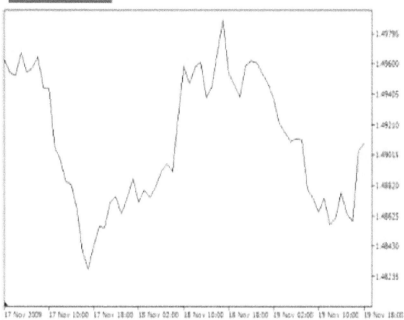

Bar Chart

Bar charts contain far more details than line charts, which are an incredibly powerful way to reflect more information regarding market fluctuations.

Similarly, bar charts connect closing prices and present opening prices simultaneously, as well as peaks and lows for the day. The top of each bar reflects the maximum price achieved during the session. The bottom represents the lowest price, and the opening and closing values respectively reflect the horizontal lines to each bar's left and right.

The duration of the bar total shows the price range for the session.

The color-coding on several charting software bars would be green to reflect an increasing price and red to represent a dropping price. For a specific session, each bar displays detail. This session's period would rely on the chart's meaning, but it may be a minute, an hour, or a day.

Main Lesson: The acronym OHLC or Free, Big, Low, and near charts are also regarded as bar charts.

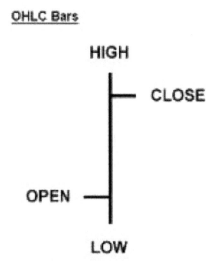

4.5 Candlestick Charts

Candlestick charts are used to visually depict details relating to the market fluctuations of a security, derivative, or currency (often known as Japanese Candlesticks). As they encapsulate a vast volume of knowledge and display it efficiently and quickly to interpret format, candlestick charts are an essential tool for Forex analytics.

Candlesticks reflect the continuum of market fluctuations over a specified period, rendering them suitable for currency technical research. Looking at an individual candlestick, the body (black or white) and the upper and lower shadows are typically used (called the wick). These upper and lower shadows represent a security's highest and lowest traded prices over the time interval shown. Opening and closing prices

Are indicated by the body. When the body is white or unfilled, the opening price is reflected by the bottom of the body and the top's closing price, as the currency closes higher than it opened. The body is black as the currency closes below the opening point, with the opening price at the peak and the closing price at the bottom.

Charting apps can also substitute colors such as red (for a lower closing) and green (for a higher closing) for the candlestick body's black or white, rendering market movements simpler to imagine.

Reading Candlesticks

Candlesticks are created from the free, large, low, and near values.

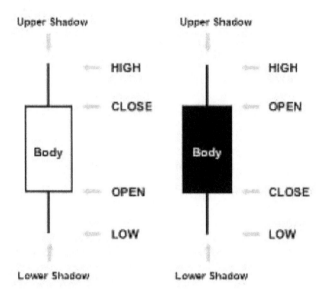

Long and Short Bodies

A long white/green body indicates a good purchasing presence. They are showing that rates have risen dramatically over the time frame. The longer the bar, the larger the increase.

A long black/red body, on the other side, indicates a strong sale presence, suggesting that prices have declined over time. Again, the greater the decrease, the longer the bar.

Long and Short Candlesticks

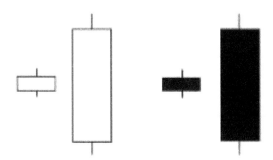

Shadows

Long shadows suggest that trading took place well above open and close rates, whereas short shadows imply that most trading took place near open and close levels.

A long upper and a short lower shadow indicate that traders attempted, but were ineffective, to drive the price higher. For candlesticks with a brief upper shadow and a lengthy lower shadow, the same is accurate.

Basic Candlestick Patterns

Candlestick maps provide a compelling way to demonstrate currency change over a specified timeline. Numerous candlestick styles can be used to evaluate the underlying consumer pattern.

White/Green Candlesticks-suggest the market's upward trajectory.

The bigger the body, the higher the average price rise.

Black/Red Candlesticks-suggest a downward business trend. Longer is the body, the more critical the price cut this period.

A Long Lower Shadow indicates a bullish sector (associated with increasing investor confidence in anticipation of future price increases). The key component of the exchange takes place at a higher profit.

A Long Upper Shadow indicates a Bearish market indicates (associated with decreasing investor confidence in anticipation of future price decreases). The key component of the exchange happens at lower price prices.

Spinning Tops are candlesticks with a comparatively narrow main body and long upper shadows and long lower shadows. Since they reflect times of indecision, the color of the body appears to be meaningless. The tiny main body indicates that markets have opened and closed within a small price range, while the long shadows mean traders have struggled to drive prices either up or down.

A white mariposa consists of a long, shadowless white body. This means that the open price is equal to the period's lowest price, and the closing price is equal to the period's highest price. It is an indicator of bullish circumstances.

The black mariposa consists of a long black body in which the open price is equal to the period high and the price at the end of the period is equal to the period low. It is a hint of bearish circumstances.

Doji-have incredibly short bodies resemble only a line, where either similar or extremely near are the open and close prices. During the time, they indicate a lack of any noticeable movement.

After a set of candlesticks with long white bodies, if a Doji forms, then this means that demand among buyers is declining. Conversely, if a dog is seen after a set of candlesticks with long black bodies, this will weaken faith among sellers.

Trends of Candlesticks

It is necessary not always to consider them as specific individuals while using candlesticks for technical study, but to see them in the sense of their surroundings. A single white/green candlestick following several black/reds alone is insufficient to show a change in trend.

However, when several white/green candlesticks begin to appear in series, this offers more valuable proof that a pattern can grow.

Various significant patterns can form within the candlestick series, each of which can be used to detect potential price trends.

We may not discuss all candlestick phenomena in detail in this report, but the following illustrations illustrate several examples of the numerous styles of candlestick patterns that may occur:

Tweezer's top trends may also be found at the close of a sustained upward or downward cycle, which shows that rates are likely to reverse. The pattern of three black crows is produced when after a previous upward trend, three successive bearish candlesticks emerge. There are signs that it is realistic to foresee a pattern turnaround.

The reverse of the three black crows is the Three White Soldiers. Typically, they emerge after a clear downward trend and indicate that there is a trend turnaround.

Main Lesson: These are only a few of the several candlestick charts that may feature in trends. There are also more, and when you improve your trading abilities, it will be helpful to research and use them. Sometimes, trend trends that use longer series of consecutive candlesticks with a higher degree of difficulty are more accurate.

4.6Ideas for discovering successful Trade Entries

Some ideas can be utilized by any dealer and by any trading strategy to seek better trade entries. For any timeline and any business, the techniques and tips mentioned here are uniformly applicable.

The Signal Size

Typically long-term chart trends composed of several candles provide a far higher predictive ability than single signals from candlesticks. We can still see all the individuals here who do not accept and assume that single pin bars create a 'killing' in the markets. However, also analysis has shown that multi-candle trends have a better predictive value.

You can seek long-term trends in trading that can easily involve 30-50 candlesticks at a time. These longer-term developments offer a lot clearer background that will tell you a whole tale of what's going on between buyers and sellers and how the two sides are changing their forces.

You may take that a step farther and not only look at the pattern itself but preferably at what occurred before shaping the pattern. Why did the tendency continue to lead through the pattern? Why the candles work, and what did is the total degree of momentum and volatility?

Factors of Confluence

A continuation of the previous one is this stage. Much like it is typically more reliable to make trading choices dependent on more candles, trading with more convergence variables will also increase your trades' efficiency.

Let the charts still say you a tale, and listen closely. The more confluence variables you have that help your exchange concept, the stronger the signal generally.

You will watch how the number of confluence variables influences your signals' precision and your overall win rate if you have a trading journal, and no trader can trade without a good journal. Until contemplating a trade with higher timeline validation and a multi-candle pattern, search for at least three convergence variables.

Of course, the form of confluence variables may differ for the trading strategy, but the underlying principle applies to all traders' styles.

Knowing the State of the Market

This argument is one that not many traders either obey or are even conscious of. As a dealer, you must know

(1) In the market conditions, the trading system works better, and then under which market conditions

(2) Choose the markets which are in such a process.

In range-bound or low movement markets, pattern traders frequently get swept up. In highly trending periods, reversal traders get fried. And range traders are running into breakout trading issues.

A completely neglected area of retail trading is business selection and understanding which market environments the approach works well.

You can take screenshots of your ten best trades right now, explore the parallels and write down the business environments under which the trades took place, and then develop the method of market selection.

Elevated Timeframes Confluence

Typically, most experienced traders believe that multi-timeframe research is faulty and does not work. We stand by it, but it's always placed in the wrong light by people.

To identify successful signs, we disagree that you would match two random timeframes. Mostly, this is complicated because it's challenging for traders to implement multi-timeframe research.

Let's stand back and remind ourselves what we intend to do with the study of various timeframes? We try to get a broader picture. We want to see where the price is compared to the long-term trend at present, whether there are broad levels nearby, and we want to make sure we get a different view.

By actually zooming out on the exact timeline we intend to trade, all this can be achieved. If we exchange the 4H timeline to find a trade, we don't go to the Regular timeframe. We remain in the timeframe of 4H. However, we zoom back. This allows one to get a precise representation of the actual scenario. Too many, we are on a very narrow timeline and ignore crucial hints. Perspective is a subject entirely ignored. Many traders remain zoomed through their one timeline and then view their charts entirely incorrectly.

Location

Let's start right away with the best entry philter. Place ensures that at or near main price ranges, you can take trades. Help and opposition, supply/demand, moving averages, Fibonacci levels, or swing highs/lows are usually those positions.

However, if they don't exist at those price ranges, the novice trader's worst problem is skipping successful trading signals. They still feel like they are losing out, and anything else seems nice about the trade, aside from the missing position requirements.

Just taking trades that exist at certain main price levels will have a significant effect on your trading over the long term since it also improves the signal strength and can also improve your efficiency.

Do you love this trade?

After accepting a poor trade that you realize you should not be in, it sucks to lose money. Then it hurts when you skip a trade that you were not optimistic about to begin with.

There's still going to be another trade, so you can't have the cashback when you make a wrong decision.

If a trade doesn't yell "amazing," and you need to weigh whether or not it's worth taking it, you're typically better off missing it.

Chapter 5: Forex Market Analysis

Creating an effective trading strategy depends on gathering market-related knowledge and the awareness of the effect on currency prices that this information may have. To evaluate the demand and pricing dynamics, this includes learning methods.

A trader's typical research forms fell roughly into three categories: Fundamental Analysis, Technical Analysis, and Market Sentiment. Everyone gives a distinct perception of market circumstances, utilizing data from a variety of sources.

5.1   Fundamental Analysis

Fundamental analysis is the method of creating and thereby manipulating the trading approach using news and intelligence items that significantly affect economic operation.

The theory behind this form of research indicates that a similarly powerful currency can usually express this performance while a nation's economy is performing well. Likewise, if a nation's economy tends to do less well, this will likely result in a weakened currency. Subsequently, this economic force's relative transfer to economies and currencies provides the foundation for speculative investing.

Fundamentals are referred to as the knowledge that forms the basis for these financial details. Fundamental data varies from macro-economic news on far-reaching world developments to more regional, national economic experience on several scales. The ultimate objective of fundamental analysis is to predict how the currency markets may be influenced by real news, stories, and data releases and decide what patterns can emerge as a consequence of these releases.

It is essential to prepare trading strategies by understanding how the market will respond to such incidents or news updates and then leverage these potential movements.

The importance of individual news events and their effect on markets differs. Large stock fluctuations will come from a response to global economic news, while the impact of less relevant details would have more subtle effects on price movements.

A vast volume of data is regularly published that can be used to schedule and handle trades efficiently. A list of the types of data to look for is given below:

- Job Tariffs

- Movements in interest rates

- Estimates for Online Transactions

- Studies on Trade Balance

- Gross Domestic Details on Goods

- Data on Inflation

- Studies on Durable Goods

Several accessible websites would provide comprehensive details about these news releases' scheduling, both in the conventional media and online. Many websites and forums online will also allow you to trigger unique alerts that will keep you aware of all essential currency-related launches.

Main Lesson: Make sure you know which weekly press releases are due. It would be beneficial to build a log of incidents that you consider might have a significant effect and then use this data to schedule potential transactions.

Trading Using Fundamental Analysis

When utilizing fundamental research, there are several essential things to learn. Generally, the influence of news on currencies is due to the discrepancy between the outcomes predicted (which are now being traded on the market) and the real results. If press data is issued that satisfies forecasts, the corresponding currency is expected to see no movement. However, if outcomes are substantially different from those predicted when the consumer responds appropriately, there is likely a heavy price movement.

There is always a quiet time in the markets before announcements as hotly awaited news reports are scheduled for publication. If the knowledge published is unpredictable and causes resulting currency market fluctuations, price adjustments are always swift and short-lived. Therefore, it is necessary to reply quickly in response to data updates while trading fundamentals.

Some economic intelligence has a more extensive business effect than others. Media reports that may have a substantial impact on the operations of the sector include:

- Rates of interest (Where interest rates are up, then currencies tend to rise accordingly).

- Estimates for jobs (Higher employment rates mean more people in work, generally reflecting a more robust economy and an equally strengthening currency).

- Domestic Gross Product (Higher GDP suggests economic resilience and a strong currency).

News reports of less significance include:

- Revenues in stores (Still a good indication of economic performance).

- Demands for Manufactured Products provides a measure of manufacturing performance. Specific considerations demand a degree of vigilance connected with the trading of fundamental knowledge.

An illustration of this is that market uncertainty frequently rises dramatically during cycles immediately after press events, contributing to rates shifting drastically over very brief periods. There may also be erratic market swings following this fast movement. These variations may result in trading orders being executed at prices that are different from what you planned, based on the execution speeds of specific brokers, when the price may adjust over the period taken to execute a deal. This condition is regarded as slippage in rates.

This instability will also trigger rates, over brief periods, to swing between gains and losses. At all moments, you should carefully watch the market and be conscious of how this trend influences your particular exchange.

Main lesson: Complete awareness of the effect of fundamentals on the sector is vital. If you are new to trading, then it is necessary to take time before trading at these moments to understand the effect of news reports, as stocks will turn in opposing directions quickly and rapidly, wiping out your gains.

Forex news schedules are issued by several websites and knowledge outlets and may reflect each one's relative relevance. It is possible to provide a precise estimate of each scheduled item's potential effect on the demand by utilizing a combination of these tools.

Fundamental Analysis – Interest Rates

One of the most important variables contributing to a currency's valuation is interest rates. An appreciation of how interest rates regulate economic growth by central banks lets a trader decide how currencies are perceived to function. Interest rate-related central bank actions are often the most relevant news stories and should still be carefully watched.

Controlling inflation is the fundamental justification for interest rate increases by central banks, which implies seeking to reduce the growth in the cost of products and services within a country. Rapid inflation implies that costs are growing too rapidly for daily products and services, commodities, etc. The purchasing capacity of commerce and the general population is being diminished.

While a degree of inflation is an agreed factor appropriate for a rising economy, it may be detrimental to economic development if inflation rises too rapidly. Central banks would then strive to preserve steady, low-level inflationary conditions with the use of interest rates.

Main lesson: In essential words, the way this is done is that central banks can always increase interest rates while inflation levels are high. This leads to more investment and less expenditure for firms and people, resulting in lower economic growth levels and minimizing inflation.

Alternatively, this helps individuals and firms spend further and invest less as interest rates are reduced, which implies more remarkable economic growth.

Trading strategy: the stronger the interest rate is operating on a given currency in Forex trading, the greater the odds of that currency improving over time. It is possible that currencies with lower interest rates would have weaker currencies.

Fundamental Analysis – Interest Rate Differentials

The differential between the interest rates of two currencies can be seen to decide whether one currency can increase and decline against another currency.

Main Lesson: The higher-yielding currency is assisted by an interest rate gap that rises, while the lower-yielding currency is supported by a disparity that decreases.

Fundamental Analysis - Example

Consideration of key central bank decisions' value is a clear illustration of how fundamental elements can affect the currency market movement. There will often be a corresponding impact on that nation's currency and all associated currency instruments when a country's central bank takes essential decisions regarding its economy.

If the European Central Bank wants to improve the conditions for promoting exports, it can opt to sell its euro holdings and purchase a currency outside the Eurozone, such as the US dollar.

The expected consequence of such a move would be a resulting decrease in the euro's value against the dollar, implying that it is easier to sell products and services to industries within the euro region. The declaration of central figures related to movements also allows markets to start pre-empting price movements, pushing stocks down, ensuring that the economy helps lower the currency value.

Main Lesson: As a Forex trader, it is crucial to be aware of announcements such as this example and consider both how the market will respond to the announcement itself in the short term and be aware of the economic repercussions in the longer term. You would recognize similar trade potential by knowing how currencies will change quickly and in the future concerning simple financial strategy.

5.2   Technical Analysis

Unlike fundamental analysis, which utilizes economic statistics and news information to forecast potential future price changes, the technical analysis method focuses on studying real market price movements to detect discernible developments and data patterns. The theory is that past pricing trends can generate a hint of potential market volatility.

The observation and study of charts plotting historical market changes is key to technical research. These provide the framework for assessing potential future currency market movements, patterns, and volatility and essential knowledge for trading strategy preparation and execution.

To evaluate the foreign exchange markets, there are several tools accessible to a Forex trader utilizing technical. The ability to map and comprehend price changes is one aspect that is central to all of these and which will shape the starting point for each phase. The aim is to understand the levels that future prices can reach by examining historical market details.

Charts may also be particularly beneficial in highlighting long and short-term developments and exposing data patterns that can be utilized to help analyze business circumstances.

In addition to the simple price display, data charts can offer several possibilities for mathematical and statistical research to be implemented, which may further expose key trends and patterns.

Identifying these chart trends is important to technical research since they explain historical, existing, and possible future price changes and underlying market factors. It is possible to schedule when and when trading trades can be conducted using them as a broker and identifying the policy behind each exchange.

Technical research is fluid in its essence, ensuring that the analysis helps break down this knowledge when circumstances shift in the marketplace (this may happen immediately or over prolonged periods). It provides a better indication of what is currently occurring and, eventually, what might arise as a consequence.

This knowledge is crucial for a trader since it helps turn arbitrary currency market movements into discernible interpretations of fundamental trends and patterns.

Several forms of technical analysis vary from methods that involve market details to detect particular trends to those that focus on statistical data manipulation to generate tools that show when and how future trading can be conducted.

A mixture of these research methods can be used for successful technical trading since this tends to minimize the chances of detecting fake patterns or false signals. Different research methods implemented to the same data can help minimize losses and improve the possibility that real trends and patterns will be correctly established.

This might all sound confusing at first sight. There are differing degrees of abilities needed to understand and adapt each strategy to regular trading operations. However, once learned and recognized, technical research can become a precious and important part of your regular trading operation.

Developing a solid understanding of the fundamentals can allow you to establish highly efficient trading techniques that will grow progressively more sophisticated over time. Each additional expertise introduces a degree of sophistication that can be implemented.

Main Lesson: A vital aspect of every market practice is considering the context and consequences of previous market fluctuations. Technical analysis offers the required daily resources to better structure and controls the where, where, and why of each and any trade transaction you produce.

5.3   Advantages of Technical Analysis

In the Forex market, technical forecasting includes technical metrics and maps to estimate a currency's price fluctuations. It has been praised as a powerful method in currency dealing by Forex traders who use technical research in their trading. On the other hand, traders who use fundamental research assume that a no-go region is technical analysis. Functional research has its advantages and drawbacks, just as there are two sides to the coin. We are going to address the advantages of technical research in the Forex sector in this report.

Psychology

Scientific research leads to the comprehension of buyers and traders' business psychology and offers a better understanding of what they do.

Price Movement

Technical research generally focuses on the consumer activity of a currency's values. Charts are used to demonstrate how markets are moving, where and the frequency of specific movements, prices are trending. The indices of oscillators, velocity, and volume provide a better scenario of market action. You may receive descriptions of market changes at a glance by using maps. Unlike fundamental analysis, where fundamentalists use economic reports, this does not extend to technical analysis. A trader will quickly make a well-measured buy or sell decision to optimize his margins by observing the action of prices of currencies on the market.

The Early Signals

The most significant benefit of technical analysis is that it gives early indications so that analysts and traders can make their decisions dependent on certain signals before reversing the pattern. With the aid of technological research, market makers' behaviors can be measured, and those activities can be observed in Price-Volume Analysis.

Easy to Find Trends

For starters, looking at a moving average, a trader can easily say if the currency's price is trending or merely trapped in a range. A map will quickly show the pattern, whether the currency is going up, down, or sideways. For technicians (technical analysts), movements are quite significant when a currency continues to shift in the direction of a certain pattern. It is simple to create these patterns using charts and make an educated and wise decision in your trading.

Information

For Swing Traders, Intraday Traders, Short Term Traders, and Long-Term Buyers, technical analysis is useful. The comprehensive details given in the technical charts allow investors and traders to take the right role in the market and to build their portfolios. With the aid of Chart Trend, Candlestick

Pattern, Uncertainty, Support, and Resistance, etc., much knowledge is given to traders and investors.

To evaluate the equity, currency, and product sector, traders and investors use a mix of different time frames to assist in the quick prediction of the market, uncertainty, and psychology of the trader.

Loads of Informative Data

Within a few seconds, technological metrics and graphs offer an abundance of details. First and foremost, it is possible to identify developments using technical analysis; volatility, sentiment, and market movements are simply and rapidly detected. There are many metrics in the Forex sector, and each offers details on different facets of currency movement. For traders to make substantial and successful transactions, this data is of vital importance.

Less Time Consuming

When using technological research in currency trading, you do not have to run complicated mathematical operations. The Internet provides a wealth of different technical metrics that a broker may use to create tremendous trading returns and accurate transactions. Compared to fundamental research, technical analysis is, therefore, less time-intensive. It is less boring and cost-effective, as well.

Easy to Identify Patterns in the Market

Market acts appear to replicate themselves unmistakably and simply. Using charts helps an investor identify trends that will help him forecast price changes, whether recent or established. Like star constellations, currency trading trends can be complicated and intricate, but it gets more straightforward with experience when you learn the craft.

Rounding tops and bottoms, head and shoulders, double and triple tops, and rising and decreasing triangles are some of the designs widely seen in the Forex industry. There are established trends that the values of currencies typically obey. In the market, they have excellent forecasting forces.

Charts say a tale regarding a currency's market movement. With multiple storylines and turns, the narrative may be complicated. On the other side, with just a few characters and a single plot, the tale may be straightforward. Only specific knowledge regarding help and resistance or patterns can be generated through technical metrics and maps. They will also have more in-depth details about how momentum builds, the intensity of a pattern, and whether the sector is evolving in a beneficial trading way.

Technical research may differentiate between substantial and successful trades and projects making losses. Use them efficiently, and you'll experience positive news during the year.

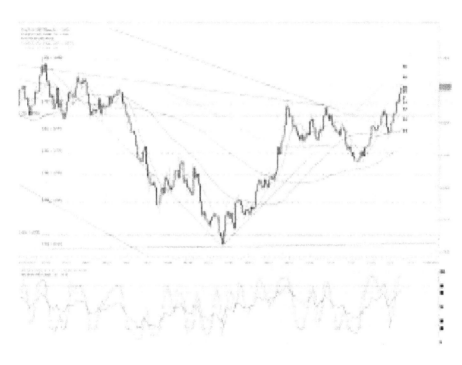

U.S. Dollar/Japanese Yen (USD/JPY), 10-minute

Market stays within 20 points of moving average

Sell entry @ 119.57

Stochastic crosses above 80

Stop out @ 118.58

Stochastics (14, 3, 3) 28.9156, 30.010

Source: Gain Capital

5.4 Fundamental Analysis v. Technical Analysis

In Forex dealing, all approaches to fundamental analysis and technical analysis are highly valuable techniques. However, although some individuals establish trading methods focused entirely on one or the other of these approaches, this is unusual. The two forms of analysis need not be mutually incompatible in the majority of situations.

Main Lesson: It is essential to consider and use all approaches to have supportive trading signals to become a profitable trader. This can indicate, in practice, technical research usage to first define the underlying currency price movements and identify patterns and signals of when and when to enter the sector.

This analysis can then be followed by utilizing the quantitative analysis to identify news outlets or market reports that offer more information to validate or refute the trading strategy. The initial study could be supported or denied by news items related to the impact of the economy for that specific currency, which could also classify important news events from the trading calendar, which may substantially affect the price change.

The odds of anything arising by mistake and destroying an otherwise credible trading plan are substantially diminished by utilizing the two forms of research together.

5.5   Market Sentiment

Although technical and fundamental assessments appear to focus mainly on raw data to assess future price changes, a good investor can often learn to consider the third form of analysis that includes attempting to determine the sector's general mood. This is the mechanism by which a trader can evaluate other traders' thoughts and emotions and try to establish a plan dependent on this community's psychology.

When preparing transactions, whether market participants are bullish or bearish is a crucial consideration. Consumer sentiment is a challenging term to quantify and grasp, but practice can eventually create the information needed to accurately gauge this sentiment.

Bulls and Bears

When traders are said to be optimistic, the word bull market applies to periods when the marketplace gives rise to greater buyers than sellers when there is significant hope. Significant price growth and substantial upward market development would always follow these conditions. By contrast, if circumstances are such that this is valid and significant pessimism among market investors, it is regarded as a bear market. It is said that traders are bearish. In general, more sellers would follow these circumstances than buyers on the market, contributing to declining rates.

5.6   Economic Indicators and their Impact on the Forex Market:

Forex and CFD (contract for difference) rates may have a pronounced impact on economic indicators. Many traders also hold a close eye on the economic calendar and ensure that they remain up-to-date for any possible uncertainty bumps lay in the road ahead.

Original Jobless Claim

This' Weekly Survey' calculated the number of individuals filing first-time applications for unemployment compensation benefits. This provides a valuable update on the labor market's intensity, particularly related to the study 'Job Condition' sample week used.

In the all-important monthly non-farm payrolls survey,' jobless claims' are a good resource to try to get a feel for future trends, but there is no precise connection between the two.

In the weekly initial jobless claims results, short-term shifts in the labor market are far more likely to be expressed than in the monthly jobs survey. Even this is one of the weekly F.X. and CFD price updates that are more impactful.

Orders for Consumer products

The Census Bureau, part of U.S., releases the Durable Goods Orders survey. To offer it its full name, the Advance Report on Durable Goods is issued about 18 business days in the month after the month for which it is registered (the day varies according to the schedule of other key releases at the time). Durable products are classified as things that are intended to last for a minimum of three years. In other terms, we usually speak of pricey goods that appear to be purchased infrequently.

This infrequency ensures that uncertainty is subject to the data, and you ought to be very vigilant with everything you learn in isolation in a single report. Analysts always omit the transport portion of the report to try to minimize this uncertainty. Another approach used is to consider a collection of reports to gauge a feeling for an overarching theme. Also, wary of changes to data from the previous month, which may be necessary?

We will continue to see new orders for durable items if demand is high and businesses have an upbeat outlook. On the other side, we would hope to see lower orders in a poor economic situation. Strength is thus bullish for risk aversion in this study, and weakness is bearish.

As far as CFD traders go, a promising indicator for stocks, all other factors are the same: resilience in durable goods. It is a common tale for the U.S. Dollar as it is for stocks in terms of the effects on the Forex market: a good study is positive for the USD. A burgeoning economy would appear to lean towards a tighter monetary policy bias from the FED.

Retail Sales

It is best defined as Retail Trade Advance Monthly Revenue. It is, though, best understood clearly as retail sales by Forex traders. The Bureau of the Census, which is a U.S. division. The Department of Commerce, at 08.30 ET, issues the paper approximately two weeks after the month in question. The survey offers an early estimation of the nominal dollar amount of retail revenue (that is, the sum is not inflation-adjusted). It records the statistic as a percentage improvement from the previous month.

It is typically this latter figure to which CFD and Forex traders respond. It is a widely watched study that can send disruptions across market rates, especially if there is a significant divergence between Wall Street's figure and expectations. Why is it a

Strongly observed text like that? It's more for saving on personal use (PCE). The PCE is a significant contributor to U.S. economic development. The Personal Income and Outlays survey from the Bureau of Economic Analysis is also worth comparing (BEA).

This explicitly involves a part of PCE, which then directly feeds into calculations of GDP. More detailed than the retail revenue data are the details covered in the report. Crucially, though, retail revenue knowledge comes out a fair couple of weeks ago, offering a more timely view into the same sector of the economy efficiently. It is an indicator of economic health if retail purchases are growing, as it appears to impact the equity market positively.

However, strong sales data can increase costs, which implies that inflationary factors need to be considered. This appears to have a favorable impact on the U.S. Currency, but it is bearish at bond rates. In comparison, the retail sales report's weakness continues to depress the equity market, bearish on the U.S. currency, but positive on bond rates.

From a research viewpoint, some components of the report can lead to unnecessary volatility. Motor vehicles appear not to be equally spread month by month because of the cost of those products. To minimize unpredictable fluctuations and interpret structural patterns in the data more readily, analysts also concentrate on automotive transactions, excluding car sales.

Utilization of Capacity

This indicator measures how the U.S. manufacturing sector performs as a percentage of maximum potential. Within a practical context, the maximum potential concept is the greatest sustainable production a factory can attain. In other terms, it brings items such as usual downtime into consideration. It is measured as an industrial demand index ratio separated by a maximum power index.

This provides us with a timely indicator of production/economic stability and an overview of developments within the manufacturing sector that could be forming. It can offer hints regarding inflation as well. It's a fair assumption that suppliers will increase rates if factories are running hot. If factories operate near their full capacity, computers are likely to malfunction due to being overworked.

In a period of intense demand, bringing computers down raises the possibility of lying off staff, which is unacceptable. Manufacturers are also able to deal with high demand by increasing costs instead of lying off staff. In exchange, this is expected to filter through to commodity costs, contributing to higher inflation. Conversely, if capacity usage is at low amounts, it is a symbol of economic decline.

As a general rule, ratings below 78% have traditionally appeared to lead to an impending recession or might also indicate that the economy is currently in recession.

As such, the FED uses this metric to assess industry developments, the broader economy, and inflation. This makes it a significant indicator, particularly for bond traders, for CFD traders to track. Still, it is also a crucial marker for those interested in the stock and F.X. markets.

Suppose you're interested in trading metrics like this, but you're not ready to start trading with your funds. Did you realize that it's possible to invest in virtual currencies without placing some of your resources at risk, utilizing real-time market data and insights from skilled trading experts? That is right.

Professional traders will evaluate their ideas and perfect them without losing their capital with a risk-free demo trading account from Admiral Markets. A demo account is an ideal spot for a novice trader to get acquainted with trading or for experienced traders to learn. Whatever the purpose might be for the modern merchant, a demo account is a must.

Factory Production Index

The Industrial Development Index calculates the degree of U.S. productivity (in terms of the volume of content generated rather than the number of dollars) in three large areas: processing, mines, and gas and electricity services, compared to the base year. The Federal Reserve compiles the paper, and it is released in the middle of each month. Any index data derives from hard data, specifically recorded from trade associations or government polls for those sectors, although this might not be accessible every month.

The FED allows calculations using proxies to fill the holes, such as hours employed from the Job Condition survey or THE volume of power utilized by the sector in question in the month. The entire index estimation procedure is laid out in the best location to search for a thorough description of the methodology involved, the 'Explanatory Sections' of the FED itself. Hundreds of components make up the index, which is then stated as the level of the index.

For starters, the Industrial Output Index preliminary release for September 2019 came in at 109.52. This is an expression, compared to the base year of the actual production. The FED used 2012 as its base cycle at the time of publication. Therefore the amount of 109.52 in September 2019 indicates that output volumes in the base frame of 2012 were 9.52 percent higher than the average level. Manufacturing makes up just about 20 percent of the U.S. economy but is closely controlled by traders of F.X. and CFDs.

The industrial sector is significant because it is responsible for most of the improvements in U.S. production seen in the business cycle, along with the construction sector, and can provide insights into the evolution of structural economic changes. The Measure of Industrial Output is procyclical.

This suggests that there is an agreement between the motions and the market cycle's shifts. For certain observers, the link between this index and economic activity is close enough to use this study as an early signal of how GDP could work.

CPI or Consumer Price Index

The CPI calculates, index-linked to a base starting point, the cost of products and services. This offers one an analytical handle on how easily markets increase or fall. Price stability is part of the FED's dual mandate, as we discussed earlier in the section. It is deemed natural or even attractive when inflation is below target ranges. However, it may have very detrimental consequences on the economy if inflation falls too far off the target for too long.

FED economists like to rely on the PCE price index presented as part of the GDP survey. This is published quarterly only, but Forex and CFD traders also obey the CPI as it is a more timely inflation tracker. There is the minimal utility of the CPI as a leading indicator for the economy.

Despite a normal and rational correlation between economic development, demand, and higher prices, it has proved to be a weak indicator of turning points in the business cycle.

High inflation was a real problem for the U.S. economy in the 1970s and early 1980s. In comparison, there was a real possibility of deflation in the wake of the world financial crisis (sustained price decreases). By motivating customers to hold off making transactions, deflation hurts the economy, so they would be cheaper in the future, as long as costs continue to decline. This would hinder economic development, which will build a negative cycle since consumer purchasing forms such a significant part of GDP.

Since inflation feeds so deeply into monetary policy, the CPI study may have a significant effect on bond, F.X., and stock market rates. It is, as usual, diversions from planned consequences that appear to have the most considerable impact. For instance, if the CPI comes in far stronger than anticipated, the FED's view is more inclined to ease monetary policy in the future may shift. This should be bullish for the U.S. Currency, all else being fair.

Similarly, such inflationary evidence could be viewed by a CFD investor as bearish for the stock market, as tighter monetary policy continues to curb risk aversion. Since the financial crash, we have remained in a very low inflationary climate, prompting the Federal Reserve to continue with a very loose monetary policy. To a degree, this has been responsible for the prolonged bull market we had in the U.S.

Federal Rate for Funds

As part of its daily timetable for deciding U.S. monetary policy, the Federal Open Markets Committee (FOMC) meets eight times a year. If there is some deviation from the planned path, the result of an FOMC meeting will significantly influence the Forex sector. The degree of interest rates in the two countries concerned and the assumptions about those interest rates are crucial factors driving Forex rates.

Suppose the Fed changes the cost of federal funding or merely changes its expectations of monetary policy's potential direction. In that case, that can make a difference to the U.S. Dollar, the world's most valuable currency. The FED offers forward guidance on monetary policy's planned course as part of the statement issued following any FOMC meeting.

This is a reasonably new measure that seeks to have more clarity as part of an attempt to reduce stock market uncertainty. As a result, monetary policy adjustments are generally announced in advance to some degree. This suggests that the forward guidance itself and the real policy adjustment have the power to impact stocks. A severe dealer in Forex or CFD would still ensure that they are informed of the FOMC Meetings Schedule.

RSI Indicator

A typical member of the "Oscillator" family of technical indicators is the "Relative Strength Index" or "RSI" indicator. To quantify the relative differences between higher and lower closing prices, Welles Wilder developed the RSI. Traders use the index to assess overbought and oversold states, useful data while setting forex market entry and exit thresholds.

As the resultant curve fluctuates between values of zero and 100, the RSI is known as an "oscillator." The indicator usually has lines drawn as warning signals at both the "30" and "70" values. Values over "85" are perceived as a strong overbought condition or "selling" signal, and a healthy oversold condition, or "buying" signal, is produced if the curve falls below "15".

RSI Formula

On the Metatrader4 trading program, the RSI indicator is normal, and the measurement formula sequence includes these straightforward steps: Choose the default length 'X' (the default value is '14', while the value '8' or '9' appears to be more sensitive;

Calculate "RS" = (Average periods of "X" up close/Average periods of "X" down close;

RSI = 100 – [100/ (1 + RS)]

Software programs do the analytical work required and create an RSI indicator. A single fluctuating curve is composed of the

RSI predictor. To increase the value of the trading signals, traders will periodically introduce an exponential moving average. The RSI is used as a "leading" predictor in that its signals predict that a pattern shift is inevitable. The flaw in the indicator is that timing is not an RSI product, the explanation for adding a moving average "lagging" to validate the RSI signal.

Large rises in price increases may lead to false signals from the RSI indicator. Complementing the RSI with another measure is wise. Wilder also assumed that the indicator's power was exposed as its rates diverged from the market's dominant prices.

Moving Average Indicator

The moving average is a metric used in technical research to reflect the stock's average trading price for a given period. Traders also allow trading averages so that the existing market momentum may be a clear indicator.

The basic moving average (SMA) and the exponential moving average are the two most widely employed moving averages (EMA). The distinction in these moving averages is that the basic moving average does not assign the averages in the data collection much weighting. In contrast, the exponential moving average offers current prices more weighting.

Formula:

The two famous moving averages are, as stated above, the simple moving average (SMA) and the exponential moving average (EMA). As a technical measure, nearly all the charting sets would have a moving average.

The basic moving average is essentially the average separated by the Number of points for all the data points in the sequence. The SMA's problem is that all data points would have the same weighting that can skew the current sector pattern's true expression.

The EMA has been created to fix this problem as it will offer the most recent prices more weighting. This makes the EMA more responsive to existing market dynamics and helps assess the course of trends.

You will find the mathematical formula for each one below:

Simple Moving Average:

SMA = (A1+A2+A3...+an)/n

Where:

A= each of the data point

N = Number of points of time

Exponential Moving Average:

$$EMA = (Vt \times (S/ (1+d) + EMAy \times [1- S/ (1+d)]))$$

Where:

d = Number of days

S =smoothing

EMAt= EMA today

Vt= Value today

EMAt= EMA today

Steps for calculation of EMA:

1. Compute the SMA for a specific time frame

2. Calculate the EMA weighting multiplier using the formula:

$[2 \div (\text{selected time period} + 1)]$. So, for a 10-day moving average, the multiplier would be $[2/ (10+1)] = 0.01818$.

3. To arrive at the current value, use the smoothing factor together with the prior EMA.

Stochastic Indicator

The Stochastic index is an indicator that calculates market momentum. And here's the method for measuring that for you math geeks out there.

%K = (Current Close – Lowest Low) / (Highest High – Lowest Low) * 100 %D = 3-day SMA of %K

Where:

Lowest Low = lowest low for the look-back period Highest High = highest high for the look-back period %K is multiplied by 100 to move the decimal point two places

MACD-Divergence with Moving Average Convergence

In all technical research, the moving average convergence divergence measure, best known as MACD (pronounced 'mac-dee'), is one of the most common instruments and has been in use since the late 1970s.

The MACD is part of the Scientific Indicators class of oscillators.

It is built to quantify a trend's characteristics. This implies its course, magnitude, and shift rate. It should also be used with the features of both its pattern following and market reversal. Two separate lines comprise the MACD. It is determined from the following three series:

The MACD series: this is the discrepancy between a "long" and a "short" EMA exponential moving average (EMA).

The EMA of the MACD series mentioned above is the "average" or "signal" series.

The discrepancy between the MACD series and the average series is the "divergence" series.

The name of the MACD stems from the moving averages on which it is centered plus how they behave. Convergence refers to the bringing together of the two moving averages. This may be viewed as evidence that a pattern shift is happening.

There may be two significations of divergence. This could imply two moving averages moving apart or that the protection pattern could be strengthened.

Divergence may also apply to a price and MACD line divergence, to which certain traders could assign importance. Suppose the price is strong when the MACD (called negative divergence" or "bearish divergence") line is falling. In that case, this could mean that the price could decline. If the market rises when the MACD line increases (called positive divergence" or "bullish divergence"), this could mean that the price could improve.

CHAPTER 6: Trading Strategy

As well as searching for market developments, the breakout is one of the components that a trader should always be looking for. Breakouts arise as a degree of support or opposition moves through the price and proceeds to travel in the same direction. As a product of several separate occurrences, this form of activity may be formed. It can appear as either a continuation of a recent trend or as the beginning of a new movement. There is also a surge in market action as real breakouts occur when traders attempt to profit on the trend, which often moves the market forward in the new direction.

They appear as a continuity breakout emerging in the direction of the previous pattern in a time of consolidation. If there is a turnaround, markets will even break down at the beginning of a new trend. Alternatively, breakouts may occur in either the upward or downward directions where thresholds vary between two bounding support or resistance levels.

To trade a breakout successfully, it is first necessary to decide if a real breakout occurs or situations that trigger false price fluctuations that may be misinterpreted as a breakout. It can help distinguish accurate breakout indications utilizing various charting methods, technological analysis, and fundamental analysis.

6.1   Trading Systems

Both trading processes function. Similarly, they should be configured to search for an emerging pattern and classify it. Automated methods should then be implemented to interpret data in a way that either confirms or disproves the original effects.

Every method can then define acceptable triggers for order entry and recommend potential benefit goals. Trade monitoring strategies can often be utilized by a scheme to help set stop losses, exit triggers, and continuously analyze the trade as it dynamically evolves. Many trading techniques are accessible, and explanations of these are simple to locate either online or from traditional tools.

Taking these concepts and then expanding on them as you gain more significant expertise is the most potent process for creating tactics and trading setups.

It is possible to decide those that best suit your specific trading style by checking individual configuration ideas in charting tools and demonstration accounts and perfecting how the setup functions in actual conditions.

Trading strategy: By taking a few basic measures, it is equally easy to create your individual and unique strategy:

1. Timeframe. The timeframe within which you will keep the exchange is necessary to settle first. This would be based on individual trading styles and aspirations for investment. Knowing this would help you to customize charting software to indicate the required timeline to monitor the exchange. Other timeframes would still need to be tracked during every transaction since they will help demonstrate what is occurring in the broader sector.

2. Find gauges that can describe a current theme. Several methods and resources can be used to recognize better and illustrate where a new pattern is emerging, as seen in this book's technological research portion. Using rolling averages will be an indication of this. Most traders will utilize a long and short moving average, and then the points at which both converge will be used to decide where new patterns are starting to develop.

3: To help validate the pattern, use markers. Suppose a potential new pattern has been established by one group of measures. In that case, it is therefore essential to attempt to validate the validity of that trend, utilizing other indicators and observational techniques. RSI, MACD, and Stochastic indicators provide descriptions of metrics that may be used for pattern validation.

4: The danger is handled. The next move is to assess the trade order that should be imposed and manage the danger associated with that order, having established a trading opportunity. This involves settling on the sum of account resources to be included, e.g., 1%, 2%, etc., and determining the future risk/reward ratios.

5: Identify/Calculate entry and exit points (triggers). Like we see in one of the main aspects of Forex trading, which essentially comes with practice, is determining when and when to join and leave trades in the earlier pieces.

It is vital to ensure that you do not enter a trade too early in the existence of a new pattern since it may prove to be a false trend, and it is not wise to leave it too late, at which time the chances of profiting have been diminished. This would rely on personal preference and expertise in terms of making the entry right.

It would eventually get simpler to spot the appropriate entry points. There are the choices of setting a trailing pause or stop loss to leave a deal, effectively closing the trade for you until the predetermined thresholds are hit. Alternatively, once the price approaches certain thresholds, you should establish clear benefit goals, likely dependent on past moves, which can again serve as escape triggers. Using help and resistance thresholds as buying or sell indicators is a widespread way of measuring exit triggers.

6: Log and follow the method. When they get interested in the exchange, one error that beginner traders often create is a failure to obey their trading method. When feelings tend to overrule sound sense, this is incredibly simple to do, but it may also be a costly mistake to produce. You realize what you plan to do and can do at - stage of the trading period by keeping to the method.

6.2   Trading Strategy

Several traders can get pulled into a breakout and continue to pursue the rapid/volatile motion when it occurs. The difficulty with this trading method is that because of the very existence of high variance. It will mean that if markets change toward your position, any earnings can be diminished quickly.

However, a far more competitive way to benefit from breakouts is to search for currency pairs where there is very little uncertainty at first. Through doing so, you allow yourself enough time to evaluate the market dynamics and the technical existence of price fluctuations and, as a consequence, set up trades that will help you to gain when a breakout happens.

This ensures that you have a greater chance to prosper from getting in at the beginning of the breakout because you can set your exchange conditions rather than attempting to pursue a breakout that is already well underway.

Measuring Volatility

To calculate the fluctuations of markets, a variety of methods may be used. Any technological measure can be used to assess the amount of market movement happening over a specified period. Both the Bollinger bands and the moving average metrics are ideal for calculating uncertainty for the technical research approaches we have previously considered.

In Bollinger bands, when there is low market uncertainty, the bands will tighten relative to the central moving average, and when there is strong price volatility, the bands will broaden away from the central moving average.

If they indicate the average price for a certain period, moving averages may also offer a clear uncertainty indicator.

Breakout Verification

Breakout signs, as described earlier, do not necessarily contribute to the creation of a true breakout case. Through time, if all these false messages were exchanged, then this would undoubtedly contribute to substantial losses. There are forms, though, to further increase the odds of detecting and verifying real breakouts. Some of the techniques mentioned earlier may be used to assess when a breakout is more probable. They may often show the degree of traction in the sector at any given period, which gives a fair indicator of where the price might be going.

A very strong measure of price and market sentiment is the moving average convergence and divergence tracker (MACD). When the histogram of the MACD is comparatively tiny, it means low momentum levels, while when the histogram of the MACD is bigger, it implies higher momentum levels.

This operates with patterns because it shows elevated traction levels and good encouragement when a trend emerges and the MACD is high. However, when in a trending situation, the MACD predictor registers low traction, this also means that support for the pattern is subsiding.

Another good indication of divergence is the relative strength index (RSI), which gives valuable insight as to whether the stock displays indicators of either being in over-bought or over-sold situations. It is also a strong indicator in all of these cases. As they arise, there could be an inevitable shift in potential trend trends.

6.3   Trading the Opposing Break

Many possible breakouts struggle to become real breakouts due to the Forex sector's dynamics; however, rates swing in the opposite direction to what was predicted. Both conditions are alluded to by many traders as a fake-out and the reverse market shift that ends in a fadeout.

The explanation for these false outs also derives from the intrinsic disparities between institutional traders' (market makers) and retail traders' trading practices (market participants). At this point, all the intricacies that contribute to this fadeout need not be identified as with time, and through practice, you can learn to recognize when and why they occur.

However, it is wise to note that they exist and that they will also occur in various markets during periods where chart trends have indicated a shift in direction. This is because institutional investors are well aware that many of the chart trends we have identified are readily recognized and utilized among retail traders.

This implies a degree of predictability in terms of what will happen in the marketplace at any given moment. Market makers will leverage this predictability to drive markets in the opposite direction of what the rest of retail participants can anticipate, resulting in a large windfall for them.

It is crucial for an inexperienced trader to be mindful of false outs and always recognize that the market will respond to what is predicted differently.

Ultimately, this understanding aims to enhance trading strategies. It suggests that an investor must ensure that when executing purchases, they utilize numerous buying signs and market measures and recognize the necessary use of stop losses and trailing stops to lock in gains and mitigate risk from any price fluctuations.

6.4 Trading Of Divergence

For every Forex investor, one of the challenges is determining when to reach the market and when to leave the market. Lock-in income needs to realize when a price will reverse and get out of a trade before that stage.

Divergence trading is one of the approaches that can enhance transactions' preparation and execution to maximize net profits. Concerning an index, divergence trading requires the comparison of real market change. The trading signal's three distinct forms may be given by indicators: crossing over the main signal line, crossing over a centerline, and diverging it.

When the real market change and a predictor are moving in different directions, indicator divergence exists. Positive variance applies to conditions when the market is in a decreasing trend, and the variable is going in the opposite upward direction (MACD, RSI, and Stochastic Oscillator). Negative divergence defines whether the price, although

The predictor shifts downwards in an upward trend.

Trading Strategy Divergence offers critical indications that signify when a pattern can begin to weaken through understanding how prices and indicators communicate. As a credible leading indicator, divergence may be used, offering trading indications that take advantage of shifts in market momentum or price path.

Two forms of divergence exist hidden divergence and regular divergence.

As an indication announcing the end of a current pattern or that a turnaround can be predicted, daily divergence is better used. In practice, this implies that even though the price tends to go up or down on the trend, the proof of divergence suggests that momentum is starting to slow down and that support for growing or declining value is beginning to decline. If the price is high, but the indicator/oscillator moves lower, this is referred to as standard bearish divergence, sometimes signaling a price streak peak. Conversely, this is regarded as normal bullish divergence, where the market tends to fall, but momentum starts to turn higher, which sometimes coincides with stocks hitting the bottom of a cycle.

Hidden separation happens within a sequence and may be seen as a cue to show that the pattern will proceed. As the real price registers increasingly higher lows, the secret bullish deviation can be observed, but the oscillator displays lower lows inconsistently. If this unique mix is discovered in an upward trend, therefore it shows secret divergence and indicates proof of continuing support for that trend.

The secret bearish variance can be shown in a declining trend, which happens as the price gradually decreases when the indicator/oscillator displays higher peaks. This may be interpreted to imply a continuation of the cycle that prevails.

Divergence - Conclusion

Differential data cannot be explicitly used to evaluate whether and when to enter transactions. Instead, they can mainly be included, among other scientific research devices, as a supporting element. It can help spot profitable times and create a better view of business trends and operations by creating an awareness of divergences in the research phase.

Scalping

Stock market securities traders sometimes use scalping to extract a comparatively modest profit on hundreds of transactions executed over a day. A dealer aims to take advantage of the discrepancies in bid/ask rates or benefit from very minor negative or positive shifts in price.

6.5   Risk Management

Trading as an economic mechanism is important to perceive and not regard as gambling. Risk control is the mechanism by which financial management strategies are utilized to guarantee that transactions are done with the approach considered and that measures are taken to decrease the risks of losing assets, thus ensuring that the risk to financial resources is reduced.

The first risk control concept is that more assets than you can expect to lose can never be traded. If the worst-case happens, most Forex day traders will begin with an account of no less than $10,000 that they can manage to risk. Although day trading is also seen as a fantastic opportunity to raise extra cash in tough times, through trading with money that they simply cannot afford to lose, many individuals have put themselves in more significant financial difficulties.

The biggest challenge is that once you are deeply involved in money trades crucial to your everyday existence, it becomes almost difficult to emotionally isolate yourself from the investing phase. This lowers the discipline of investing, which will potentially result in poor investment decisions.

Education is the next fundamental step in risk control. Before making any transaction backed by real financial wealth, the more informed, you will be, the stronger the likelihood of success moving forward. Reading tools like this and other titles can also provide the Forex industry with a detailed context and illustrate the peculiarities found in everyday trading.

It can help avoid errors or misinterpretations by getting an explicit working knowledge of how the business works and the particular language used among market participants. To create, comprehend, and perfect techniques and configurations before sacrificing money, it is often advisable to use demonstration accounts and demonstration tools extensively.

There is a wealth of online and offline outlets that will help to understand Fore's technique. Several resources are available to help fast-track the Forex learning path to obtain admission to mentors or tuition. Many of these may be immensely helpful as they provide people with real Forex trading expertise the ability to benefit directly from them. It is possible that these services would be relatively expensive, so it is necessary to understand the advantages they may offer against the needed capital outlay.

6.6   Stop Loss

In contrast to all of the research and trading methods presented in this text, we have proposed how stop-loss orders can be used. For any Forex trader, stop loss is an incredibly useful method since it allows you to schedule transactions and conduct selling or buying orders and can be used to simplify the trading phase while you are inaccessible. Your usage of stop losses and your unique trading strategies should represent market conditions.

In any trade you perform, they should be included. When putting stop losses, it is necessary to recognize a variety of factors:

1. A stop loss should not be put above or below your entry point too closely. This is because, except in a trending economy, stocks can still fluctuate up and down to a certain degree. If the stop loss is closely fixed to the market, then these swings will quickly trigger the trade to close prematurely.

2. Likewise, stop losses should not be placed too far from the points of entry. With practice, having the proper equilibrium on where to set stop losses can increase.

3. Stop losses cannot be precisely placed on assistance or resistance thresholds. Instead, these thresholds can be used as indicators from which stop losses may be placed either above or below these locations. Since markets appear to move into stages of help and resistance, this would prevent any exchange from closing early due to market volatility.

CHAPTER 7: Forex Specifics (Exit Strategies, Trend lines & Time frame)

- Volatility based approach using ATR

- Moving average trailing stops

- Traditional stop/limit (using support and resistance)

Traders spend a lot of their energies on spotting the right opportunity to enter a deal. Although this is critical, it is essential to leave transactions that will dictate how efficient the exchange is. This hones in on three exit trading tactics that traders can remember when trying to get out of a deal.

STRATEGY #1: Volatility Based Approach Using (ATR)

The Average True Selection is used by this final technique (ATR). The ATR is structured to calculate uncertainty in the business. Through taking the average range over the last 14 candles between the high and the bottom, it shows traders how volatile the market is doing, and this can be used for each transaction to establish stops limits.

The higher the ATR is on a single pair, the larger the stop must be. This makes sense because it might stop a close stop on an unpredictable pair too soon. Setting stops that are too large for a less risky pair often takes on more risk than required, ultimately.

As it can be adjusted to any period, the ATR predictor is standard. Set your stop marginally above 100% of the ATR and set at minimum the same distance away from the entry point to establish your limit.

STRATEGY #2: Moving Average Trailing Stops

A moving average has long been considered a powerful method to filter what path a currency pair has trended in. The fundamental premise is that when the market is over a moving average, traders search for purchasing opportunities. When the price is below a moving average, they look for selling opportunities. It may also be helpful, though, to view a moving average as a trailing stop.

The principle is that if an M.A. crosses the price, the pattern changes. Once this transition has happened, pattern traders will want to close out the positions. This is why it may be beneficial to set your stop loss depends on a moveable average.

STRATEGY #3: Traditional STOP/LIMIT (Using Support and Resistance)

One of the most straightforward strategies to hold feelings in line is establishing expectations (limits) and avoiding the same moment as the exchange is entered into. This is a lot safer plan than joining without a 'stop-loss' and trying to rub the sweat off your forehead while you see the account collateral consumed by failing trades.

It is noticed that establishing a risk to reward ratio of at least 1:1 was one of the typical characteristics of active traders across daily's analysis into over 30 million live trades.

Traders should analyze the danger they can assume and set a stop at that stage before making an entrance into the sector, thus setting a goal at least that many pips away. Trades are automatically stopped at an appropriate amount of danger if traders are wrong; if traders are right, and the price meets the target, the deal is automatically closed. Any result presents an escape for traders.

Traders seeking to go long will search for price combined with simple buying signals utilizing indications to bounce off help. As prices have briefly broken below support, traders will look to stop marginally below the support level. As the price has approached this amount many times, the cap may be set at a resistance level. This can be changed for short positions, and stops may be positioned near resistance with limitations placed on assistance.

7.1 Trend Line

You recognize that Support and Resistance are horizontal areas that indicate future buying/selling pressure on your graph. And for Trend

Line, it's the same. The main distinction is that the Trend Line is not horizontal but sloping.

Upward Trend Line: "Sloping" region that indicates upward spending pressure on the graph.

Downward Trend Line: On the graph "Sloping" region indicates downward selling pressure.

Trading Strategy for Re-Entry

A high likelihood trading term is re-entry trading.

7.2   Time Frames for Forex Trade

Often traders do not consider the real-time period they intend to sell or how long they plan to keep a place. They will set a stop loss and take benefit order amounts, but they do not have a specific period in mind to close their position otherwise.

Three basic Time Frames for Trading

Many traders and observers would accept that three large groups may be divided into trading time frames. Typically, these time frames are defined as the short, medium, and long term time spans.

The first point relevant to remember regarding this concept is that among forex traders, other financial market observers, and writers, each time frame definition does not have a specific meaning.

Perhaps the easiest explanation to understand this difference is that considering the sort of trading technique that a dealer uses, the time intervals these widely employed words apply to appear to focus on the average time a position is held.

Therefore, if a trader uses a trading technique that appears to have a comparatively short holding period, such as a day trading strategy, where all positions are closed by the end of the trading day, the duration of time-correlated with each time frame word would be proportionately less than the length of time. For example, a swing or pattern trader might retain positions for a trader.

7.3   Forex Time Frames Trading Strategy

Although the market period's language is not particularly specific, it may also help obtain a general interpretation of what terms such as long term, medium-term and short term generally refer to traders utilizing various trading techniques.

For instance, it is possible to explain how each of these definitions seeks to encompass the most appropriate day traders. Who typically aim to end trading positions on the same day they were started and therefore typically do not retain positions overnight:

The Long Term-This time cycle spans a span from few hours to a full-day session for a day trader.

The Medium Term-This time range spans ten minutes to about an hour for a day trader.

The Short Term-This time spans a period from seconds to several minutes for a day trader.

On the other hand, Swing traders look to reap the benefits of broader market exchange rate variations. Typically, they are more than ok with keeping roles overnight. Each of these time frame groups appears to encompass the time span that is most applicable to swing traders. The following can be described:

The Long Term-This swing trader time horizon spans a span ranging from few months to a year or more.

The Medium Term-This swing trader time span crosses the extent of many weeks to a month or so.

The Short Term-This swing trader period spans a very short duration lasting from a couple of days to a week.

Finally, those involved in long-term trading in foreign exchange patterns or investing operations of foreign currencies appear to have a much longer period over which they can retain positions.

The Long Term-This time spans a duration spanning a few months or more than a few years for pattern traders or buyers.

The Medium-Term- This period spans a few weeks or as much as a few months for pattern traders or buyers.

The Short Term- This time spans a duration of a few weeks for pattern buyers or buyers.

Trading Countertrend

Countertrend trading is a form of swing trading method that believes that it can change a current market pattern and seeks to benefit from that reversal. In particular, countertrend investing is a medium-term tactic in which positions are kept for many days or several weeks.

To make their judgments, countertrend traders depend on envelope networks (such as Bollinger Bands), indicators (such as the Aaron Indicator), and oscillators (such as the Relative Strength Index or Chand Momentum Oscillator). For several reasons, including pure benefit, diversification, and risk management, traders can use countertrend strategies.

Strategies for Countertrend Trade

Countertrend trading policies are confusing and are thus usually used mainly by advanced traders. They should use diversification and risk control or forward-looking estimates.

Diversification and Risk Management

Active traders are conservative of their portfolio that they lose with each deal; a well-known standard in the sector is the 2 percent law. Usually, advanced active traders operating according to technical signals would devise grid trading policies.

The strategies position small trading bets during a trend to control their risk, defined at intervals when the price rises or decreases. Conceptually, countertrend grid methods that take opposite roles may also help mitigate danger for traders.

Several competing successful traders chose to concentrate entirely on a countertrend trading approach. Such traders assume that a rebound will pay off by purchasing (rather than selling) in a bearish downtrend. In an attempt to theoretically capture a turnaround in the pattern, they can even take short positions in an uptrend rather than investing.

Forward-looking Predictions

When an investor tries to take countertrend positions at resistance or support price points in the future, another form of countertrend approach more similar to swing trading may be applied. This style involves betting that the paradigm will change to a different path, and their positions will prosper accordingly.

A forward-looking countertrend strategy also needs the advanced usage of conditional orders. Conditional orders enable an investor to designate a sale price near levels of opposition or a purchase price near help levels. Advanced conditional orders allow an investor to specify a profitable price using both regular orders and choice orders.

Therefore, it is necessary to program advanced conditional instructions as bracketed orders enforced when a turnaround happens and provide higher and lower requirements to control future benefit and loss.

How to Determine Position Size When Forex Trading

Your location size, or exchange size in units, is more important than your entry and exit points while exchanging currency (Forex) prices on a day. You may have the most robust forex plan in the world, but you can either take too much or too little risk if your trade size is too large or tiny. And losing so much will quickly vaporize a trading account. The number of lots and the amount and sort of lot you acquire or offer in a trade decide the position size:

A micro lot is a currency comprising 1,000 units.

10,000 units is a mini-lot.

100,000 units are the default lot size.

Your risk, trade risk, and account risk are broken down into two pieces. Here's how both of these components come together to give you the optimal size of position regardless of what the business dynamics are, what the trading setup is, or what technique you use.

Set the limit of risk per trade for your account

This is an essential move in assessing the scale of the forex role. Set a percentage or dollar sum cap on each exchange that you'll lose. For instance, if you have a $10,000 trading account, if you use the 1 percent cap, you could lose $100 per transaction. If the risk cap is 0.5 percent,

So $50 a transaction will be risky. The amount of your account and the overall number you calculate will still determine the dollar cap. For any trade you make, this cap becomes your rule.

You should also use a set dollar number, which can also be 1% or less of your account's worth. You could be losing $75 per exchange, for instance. As long as the account balance is $7,500 or higher, 1 percent or less would be at risk.

Account risk should be kept stable while other trading variables can alter. Don't gamble 5% on one trade, 1% on the next, and 3% on another. Choose and continue with the percentage or dollar sum until you reach a stage where the dollar amount you have picked hits the 1 percent percentage cap.

The Pip Risk Plan for Trade

You should switch your mind to the transaction in front of you now that you know the full account danger on any trade. The distance between the entry point and the point where you put your stop-loss order decides the pip chance for each exchange. A pip, which is short for "percentage in point" or "price interest point," is usually the smallest component of a shifting currency price. A pip is 0.0001, or one-hundredth of a percent, for most currency pairs. A pip is 0.01, or 1 percentage point, for pairs that contain the Japanese yen (JPY). Any brokers plan to view rates with one additional decimal position. The fifth decimal position (or eighth, for the yen) is called a pipette.

When it losses a certain sum of capital, a stop-loss order locks out a deal. That is how you guarantee that the loss does not surpass the loss of account risk, and its position is often dependent on the trade pip risk. So, for example, you lose 10 pips if you purchase a EUR/USD pair at $1.2151 and place a stop-loss at $1.2141. Dependent on uncertainty or policy, pip risk differs. A trade can often have five pips of risk, and there may be 15 pips of risk for another trade.

The next move is to measure the pip value based on the lot size until you know how far away your entry point is from your stop failure in pips.

Understand Pip Value for a Trade

The pip rates for various sizes of lots are fixed whether you are exchanging a currency pair. The U.S. dollar is the secondary currency, named the quote currency, and your trading account is supported with dollars. The pip worth is $0.10 for a micro-lot, It's $1 for a mini-lot, and it's $10 for the default lot.

You will have to multiply the pip amounts by the currency exchange rate for the dollar vs. your quote currency if dollars finance the trading account and the quote currency in the pair you are trading is not the U.S. dollar. Let's assume the euro/British pound (EUR/GBP) pair is being exchanged, and the USD/GBP pair is trading at $1, 2219.

The pip worth will be $0.12 ($0.10 * $1.2219) for a micro-batch of EUR/GBP.

That will be $1.22 for a mini lot ($1 * $1.2219)

That will be $12.22 ($10 * $1.2219) for a regular lot,

The position size is the only factor left to measure now.

Determine the size of position for a transaction

It is possible to determine the optimal position size using the equation below:

Risk pips * pip value * lots traded = volume at risk

The position size in the formula above is the number of lots exchanged.

Let's say you have a $10,000 portfolio, that with each deal, you lose 1 percent of your account. So the overall risk level is $100 for each transaction. You're trading the EUR/USD pair, and you determine that at $1, 3051, you want to purchase and put a $1, 3041 stop loss. This means you put 10 pips ($1, 3051-$1, 3041= $0.001) at danger. Each pip motion has a worth of $1 because you've been dealing in mini lots.

If you plug a number into the equation, you can get:

10*$1* lots exchanged = $100 * lots traded

If you divide the equation's two sides by $10, you can arrive at:

Trading lots = 10

Although 10 mini lots equal one regular lot, either 10 mini lots or one standard may be bought. Now let's go to a scenario in which you're selling EUR/GBP mini lots, and you plan to purchase at $0.9804 and put a $0.9794 stop loss. That's 10 pips of chance again.

10 * $1, 22 * lots exchanged = $100 * lots traded

Note, in section three, the $1.22 meaning arises from our conversion formula above. This figure will differ based on the actual rate of trade between the dollar and the British pound. If you split the formula by $12.20 for both ends, you arrive at:

Trading lots = 8.1919

So eight mini lots and one micro lot should be your place size for this exchange. Along with the 1 percent law, you are well prepared to measure your forex trades' lot size and location with this method in mind.

7.4 Market Expectations

When it comes to forecasting how the market will adapt to data releases or market developments or why it responds the way it does, there is no simple "All in or "Bet the Farm" recipe for success.

You should rely on the idea that an initial reaction usually occurs and is generally short-lived but full of activity. The second response, where forex traders have had some time to think about the news's effects or report on the existing market, arrives later.

At this stage, the market determines whether the press statement went along with or against the current assumption. And whether it responded appropriately. Was the report's result predicted or not? And what does the market's initial reaction tell us about the broader picture? Answering such questions offers one a position to continue to understand the market activity that follows.

7.5 Consensus Market Expectations

The relative agreement on future economic or news projections is a consensus expectation, or simply consensus. Various leading economists from banks, investment companies, and other securities-related organizations are creating economic predictions. By observing her in-house analyst and the array of financially sound "players" on the sector, your favorite news celebrity gets into the mix.

All the projections are pooled and summed together, and it is these averages show on charts and calendars. They represent the degree of anticipation for the document or occurrence.

The consensus becomes ground zero; this baseline figure compares the incoming or real results. Incoming data is usually defined in the following manner:

"As expected"-the details published was similar to the consensus estimate or above it.

"Better-than-expected" was more than better than the consensus estimate for the published results.

"Worse-than-expected" was much worse than the consensus estimate for the published results.

A significant evaluation for evaluating price behavior is whether incoming data reach agreement or not. The assessment of how much better or worse the real data is in the majority prediction is just as significant. Larger degrees of inaccuracy raise the risk and the extent to which the price can adjust after the report is out.

Let's note, though, that forex traders are knowledgeable and can be ahead of the curve. Ok, anyway, the nice ones. Many forex traders have already "priced in" consensus expectations long before the study is planned in their trading and the business, let alone published.

As the name suggests, pricing applies to traders who have a vision of a case's result and make bets on it before the news comes out. The more probable a story is to adjust the market, the faster markets can price in the opinion assumptions. How do you know if the new demand is the case? Yeah, that one is difficult.

You can't tell, but when a study is published, you have to take it on yourself to keep on top of what the market commentary suggests and what price activity is doing. It can provide you an indication of how high the business has cost. Before a report is released, a lot can happen, so keep your eyes and ears open.

Just before a publication, consumer mood may change or worsen, so be mindful that prices can respond with or against the pattern. There is always the probability that data analysis is utterly missing goals. So don't bet on the expectations of anyone away from the farm. You'll be sure to see market movement arise as the miss happens.

Help yourself out by expecting it and other potential outcomes) to happen in such a case. Play the game "what if." Tell yourself,

"What if A occurs?" What if B occurs? How would traders respond to their bets or adjust them?"

You might be more descriptive, still. What if half a percent of the study was supposed to come in? How far pips down are stocks going to move? With this study, what will need to happen that could trigger a 40 pip drop? Something? Come up with multiple scenarios and be prepared to respond to the answer of the sector. In this way, being strategic will hold you ahead of the game.

7.6   What is the best time to trade Forex?

This query is meant specifically for day traders.

It doesn't matter the right moment to trade the Forex market, whether you're either a swing trader or sole trader or trade the longer timeline. And to you, it is meaningless. But if you're a short-term trader (day trading), it's essential to know the right period for Forex trading.

London Session

For traders who wish to deal in uncertainty, the strongest session in London is then. That during trading hours, you have the highest amount of trades and fluctuations.

Overlap Session London and New York

The perfect time to exchange is for London and New York to coincide, to be even more specific. Today is the ideal opportunity to exchange, which ensures the London and New York sessions are available at the same time!

What's the perfect day for forex trading?

There are some perfect days to sell Forex, much like the ideal day to trade Forex within those hours! It's Tuesday, Wednesday and Thursday, commonly speaking.

CHAPTER 8: Forex Money Management: Trading and psychology

Some forex traders lose, and others win money while utilizing the same Forex approach. Why is it occurring? The truth is that trading on the stock market is viewed by experienced traders as a job and not as a gambling game. The secret to achieving profitability in Forex is consistency in trading. You ought to maintain care of your thoughts and obey the laws of money management to do this.

Inexperienced traders view forex trading as fun and quick currency, but they don't sit here for a long time. They lose it and their total capital after earning a random, fast profit and then retire from trading forever. No wonder they claim that on Forex, no more than 10% of traders gain. Since, first of all, Forex is a grueling job for yourself, the methodology and risk management. Because of the large leverage scale, Forex trading is deemed the most lucrative and the riskiest way to earn money. The trader is thus bound to loss without dealing with the fundamental principles of money management.

The probability of winning is a little less than 50 percent if you equate Forex trading with playing roulette, then gambling on black or red. The likelihood decreases accordingly if you bet on a particular number. A trader may individually regulate the expectation of benefit during Forex trading. For this, an acceptable cost and benefit combination has to be achieved. This will only be achieved if there is a policy, a negotiating plan, and accordance with Forex money management laws, mitigating the effect of the trader's two key issues on the outcome of the transaction: uncertainty and greed. Fear causes you, when the first failure happens, to close a spot. Greed contributes to a lucrative contract being negotiated in advance, keeping you from achieving the best potential profit. You must take care of your feelings and behave solely in line with your trading strategy if you want to thrive in Forex.

The psychology of investing is that the market's minimum gains are more readily viewed and do not wipe out the dealer. It is also critical that the future losses from a single transaction do not surpass 2-3% of your deposit and that the benefit anticipated is at least twice the size of the stop loss. You can recognize that no trading scheme will be without drawdowns, but even a few losing trades in a row would not contribute to substantial losses and can be compensated by gains in the future if you do not misjudge the risks.

8.1 Basic Money Management Principles for Trading

Money management laws appear clear and banal at first sight, but not everyone obeys them, thus the sad numbers of traders who have lost their savings. Write down these laws and position them in a prominent location on a sheet of paper, let them always warn you how to sell, and then you can never risk your savings.

Never trade in some capital you can't afford to risk. And if you discover a trading plan, you're entirely confident that you don't want to take out a loan, sell a property, or exchange for cash. Trading is a very dangerous earnings instrument. Progress can only come to you if you are equipped psychologically for future losses;

Always use a stop loss. You must determine the potential losses before starting a deal to assess whether to join the trade and how much. Trading without stops is a roulette game, which will lead you to fail sooner or later;

In a single deal, never lose more than 2 percent of the investment. Trading on the Breakeven Forex is a fallacy. Without defeat, no plan is successful. These losses must be under your power. Your deposit must survive any drawdowns if you exchange with minimum harm, and potential gains would override prior losses;

At least 2-3 times the stop loss could be the take-profit size. You will easily recover the previously acquired losses with this strategy and get a plus;

When to unlock a contract and when to lock it, you need to know precisely. That is, you have to have a schedule for trading and still adhere to it. In making simple, yet precise and careful decisions, forex trading should be systematic.

Glossary

200 AUS:

A word for the Australian Securities Exchange (ASX 200) is an index of the largest 200 firms listed on the Australian stock exchange (by market capitalization).

Accrual

Allocation, for the course of each negotiation, of rates and discounts on forwarding trading trades specifically linked to deposit swap (interest arbitrage) agreements.

Adjustment

Official intervention typically culminated in an adjustment either in the internal economic policy to fix the disparity of payments or the official currency rate.

Barrier Level

The arrangement of a Barrier Choice requires a certain price of considerable significance. The conditions of a particular Barrier Option allow for a sequence of incidents to arise if a Barrier Threshold price is met.

Base Currency

The first currency in a pair of currencies. This explains how much the base currency is worth against the second currency as calculated. For e.g., if the rate of USD/CHF (U.S. Dollar/Swiss

Franc) equals 1.6215, then CHF 1.6215 is worth one USD. The U.S. dollar is generally called the base currency for quotes in the forex industry. Implying quotes are represented as a unit of USD 1 per other currency quoted in the pair. The British pound, the euro, and the Australian dollar are the main exceptions to this law.

Price Bid

The amount that the public is prepared to consume a commodity. Prices are quoted as bid/Ask, two-way. In F.X. trading, the offer is the price at which the base currency, seen to the left in a currency pair, may be offered by a dealer.

For instance, the base currency is USD in the quotation USD/CHF 1.4527/32, and the offer price is 1.4527, which implies that for 1.4527 Swiss francs, you can sell one U.S. Dollar. In CFD dealing, the bid often illustrates the price at which a trader will offer the commodity. For example, in the quote for UK OIL 111.13/111.16, the auction price is £ 111.13 for one unit of the underlying demand.

Broker

For a fee or commission, a person or company serves as an intermediary, putting together buyers and sellers. By comparison, a broker contributes resources and takes one side of a role, aiming to gain a spread (profit) by closing the position with another party in a corresponding exchange.

Candlestick Chart

A map that displays the day's exchange spread as well as the price of opening and closing. The rectangle between the open and close prices is shaded whether the open price is greater than the close price. If the closing price is greater than the open price, there is no shading in that region of the graph.

Carry Trade

A market technique captures the disparity between the interest rates paid from a currency that pays a reasonably high-interest rate for an extended period versus a currency that pays a lower interest rate for another currency. For starters, for some time, the NZD/JPY (New Zealand Dollar/Japanese Yen) has been a widespread carry trade. The elevated yielder is NZD, and the medium yielder is JPY. Traders are purchasing NZD and selling JPY, or being long NZD/JPY, will be trying to take advantage of this interest rate gap. The carry trade is said to be unwinding as NZD/JPY starts to downtrend over a prolonged period, most possibly owing to a change in interest rates.

Day Trader

Before the end of the same trading day, speculators take positions in products and later liquidate certain positions.

Dealer

A person or business operating as a principal or a transaction counterpart. One side of a role is taken by principals, aiming to gain a spread (profit) by closing the position with another group in a corresponding exchange. In comparison, a broker is a person or company who serves as an agent for a fee or commission, bringing together buyers and sellers.

Extended

A market which is assumed to have gone too fast, too soon.

Follow-Through

Following a directional break from a specific price level for a new buying or selling, interest is called "follow-through." Typically, the absence of follow-through indicates that a directional move will not be sustained and may reverse.

Fundamental Analysis

Evaluate all the relevant knowledge on a tradable good to decide its potential prospects and forecast where the price is going. In fundamental research, sometimes non-measurable and arbitrary judgments, as well as quantifiable measurements, are made.

Last Dealing Day

You can exchange a special item on the last day.

Last Dealing Time

You can exchange a specific item for the last time.

Leverage

This is the proportion or fractional raise you will exchange from the sum of money you have available, often known as margin. It makes it possible for traders to trade notional values far higher than their capital. For e.g., 100:1 leveraging implies that an abstract asset can be exchanged 100 times more than the money in your trading account.

Limits /Limit Order

A request that aims to acquire at prices lower than the current market or offer at levels more significant than the current market. A cap order imposes a limit on the actual amount to be charged or the minimum price to be received. For e.g., if USD/JPY's current price is 117.00/05, then the maximum order to purchase USD will be at a price below the current market, e.g., 116.50. A Restriction Order added to a current open position (or a pending admission order) can be referred to as a "Take Profit" order for the intention of closing the position.

Market Makers

A trader who quotes both offers and asks rates daily and is prepared to establish a two-sided demand for every financial commodity.

Order Book

A method used to demonstrate the breadth of sellers' demand ready to purchase and sell beyond the best possible rates.

Paid

Refers to the business dealing side of the sale.

Pair

The convention of comparing one currency to the other in the forex quotation.

Shorts

Traders who have sold a stock or shortened it or others that are bearish on the market.

Technical Analysis

The method of analyzing maps of historical market trends seeking hints as to possible price fluctuations.

Variation Margin

To deal with market volatility, fund traders must keep in their accounts the appropriate margin necessary.

Yard

Billions of units.

Yield

The return percentage on an investment.

Conclusion

Overall, this book's purpose was to include an overview of the Foreign Exchange Markets and provide you with the resources required to begin trading. One essential lesson to be learned is that there is sadly no 'complete configuration' or 'super technique' that will succeed every time.

While several books and blogs tend to claim otherwise, claiming that their setup is the road to 'guaranteed income,' the fact remains that there are no promises regarding trading. Markets are not just numerical movements but are complex manifestations of human behavior and the actors in the business. This, combined with the complexities in forecasting the future, renders it problematic for a single calculable equation to minimize the threats, where the results are reliably correct.

Main Lesson: You can often find yourself on the wrong side of the game. Business and unfair decision-making. It's not a negative thing here.

It is essential to benefit from failures and use them to help increase the likelihood of more successful potential decisions.

A comprehensive overview of the Forex markets or Forex dealing is by no way this novel. Instead, the aim was to provide you with the requisite knowledge to recognize how the markets operate and to describe some of the methods and strategies that can be used to start preparing and make trades. Ultimately, the trading method can be a constant learning curve, offering fresh perspectives and new ideas about benefiting from an efficient and ineffective exchange.